ONE THING AND ANOTHER

ONE THING
AND ANOTHER

by
HILAIRE BELLOC

A Miscellany
from his Uncollected Essays
selected by
PATRICK CAHILL

LONDON
HOLLIS & CARTER

PRINTED AND BOUND IN ENGLAND BY
HAZELL WATSON AND VINEY LTD
AYLESBURY AND LONDON FOR
HOLLIS AND CARTER LTD
25 ASHLEY PLACE, LONDON, SW1

First published 1955

IN MEMORY
OF ONE
WHO SPOKE THE TRUTH, AND
CALLED THINGS BY THEIR RIGHT NAMES

ACKNOWLEDGEMENTS

THE Editor offers his thanks to all those who have assisted in the production of this book and, in particular, makes due acknowledgement to the editors and publishers of the following journals and books in which these essays first appeared:

The New Statesman (for Nos. 1, 4, 6, 10, 14, 18, 23, 26, 29), *The London Mercury* (3), *The Outlook* (7, 15), *The New Witness* (9, 11, 12), *The Universe* (13, 24), *The Geographical Magazine* (16), *G. K.'s Weekly* (17, 25, 27, 31, 32, 35), *Country Life* (19, 20), *The English Review* (22), *Wine and Food Quarterly* (28), *The Tablet* (30), *Life and Letters* (33), *The Weekly Review* (36), *Daily News* (38), *In Autumn's Sickle*, Elkin Mathews Ltd. (2), *Imaginary Biographies*, George Allen & Unwin Ltd. (5), *The Footpath Way*, Sidgwick & Jackson Ltd. (8), *The Fame of Blessed Thomas More*, Sheed & Ward (21), *Sussex, The Resistant County*, The Homeland Association Ltd. (34), *The New Keepsake*, R. Cobden-Sanderson Ltd. (37).

The bibliographical search for the material from which these essays have been selected was encouraged by the interest of Mr. J. J. Sullivan, Mr. C. F. Petelle and the Reverend Silvester Humphries, O.P., for whose assistance I am deeply grateful.

P. C. C.

CONTENTS

[The Editor's notes which appear at the head or foot of some of the essays have been kept as brief as possible, and the individual dates of the essays, which belong to the period 1911–41, have been stated only when they were deemed significant.]

I

BY WAY OF PREFACE

An Essay upon Essays upon Essays

THERE has been a pretty little quarrel lately—it will probably be forgotten by the time this appears, but no matter—a quarrel between those who write essays and those who have written an essay or two to show that the writing of essays is futile. These last seem to be particularly annoyed by the foison of essays in the present generation. They say it has burst all restraint and is choking us under a flood.

Of old, the essay appeared here and there in some stately weekly paper. Then it dignified once a week some of the more solemn of the daily papers. Then it appeared in another, and another more vulgar. Then, not once a week, but twice a week, in these last: finally, every day. And now (say they) it is everywhere. And the enemies of the essay—or at least of this excess of essays, this spate of essays, this monstrous regiment of essays—are particularly annoyed by the gathering of the same into little books, which they think a further shocking sin against taste. It is bad enough (they say) to drivel away week by week, or even day after day, for your living, but you may be excused (poor devil!), for a living you must get. What is quite unpardonable is to give this drivel the dignity of covers and to place it upon shelves.

The enemies of the modern essay go on to say that it cannot possibly find sufficient subject-matter for so excessive an output. And so on.

Now here let me break modern convention at once, and say that I am a good witness and in a good position also to plead in the matter. I have written this sort of essay for many weary years. I know the motive, I know the method, I know the weakness, but also all that is to be said for it. And I think that, upon the whole, the modern practice is to be supported.

I certainly do not say that with enthusiasm. It would be better for literature, no doubt, and for the casual reader (who reads a great deal too much), if the output were less. It would certainly be better for the writer if he could afford to restrict that output. But I know that, in the first place, the level remains remarkably high in this country (where there are a dozen such things turned out to one in any other), and that it does so remain high is an argument in favour of the medium. For a sufficient standard maintained in any form of writing should be proof that there is material and effort sufficient to that form: that there is a need for that form to supply, and that it is supplied.

These modern essays of ours may be compared to conversation, without which mankind has never been satisfied, which is ever diverse (though continually moving through the same themes), and which finds in the unending multiplicity of the world unending matter for discussion and contemplation. It lacks the chief value of conversation, which is the alternative outlook—the reply. That cannot be helped. But I fancy the reader supplies this somewhat in his own mind, by the movements of appreciation or indignation with which he receives what is put before him. Indeed, sometimes his indignation moves him to provide free copy in protest; though I am afraid that the corresponding pleasure does not get the same chance of expression. I do indeed note, especially in the daily papers nowadays, continual letters from correspondents approving (usually) the more horribly commonplace pronouncements, or those which have been put in to order, as part of some propaganda or other undertaken by the owner of the sheet. These letters I suspect. I believe they are arranged for. But the letters of indignation are certainly genuine, and editors get a good many more than they print. When such letters are written in disapproval of what I myself have written, I nearly always agree with them.

I can also claim to give evidence as a reader of other people's essays. For I can read this kind of matter with less disgust than any other in the modern press. Yes, I prefer it even to murders. And I cannot tell you how much I prefer it to ignorant comment upon the affairs of Europe or conventional rubbish upon affairs domestic: the presentation of little men as great, of falsehood as truth, of imaginaries as realities.

As for a dearth of subject, I see no sign of it at all. If I consider any one man of that half-dozen or so whom I read regularly, my colleagues in this same trade, I can name no one except myself who tends to repetition. And there is no reason why a fairly well-read man, still active and enjoying occasional travel, let alone the infinite experience of daily life, should lack a subject. Stuff is infinite. The danger lies not in the drying up of matter but in the fossilization of manner. Nor do I find much trace of *that* in my contemporaries.

I have, indeed, the contrary fault to find with the English essay to-day, and that is the restriction of matter. There are whole departments of the highest interest to man which are, by convention, avoided. For instance, until quite lately (when the ice was courageously broken by one group of newspapers), a discussion of the ultimate truths and of whether those truths could be discovered or stated—in other words, a discussion of what is generically called "religion"—was forbidden. Now that the ice *has* been broken, editors have discovered—a little to their astonishment, I think—that the pioneer was right—that there is nothing for which the public has a stronger appetite than theology.

Another form of restriction is the absence of a devil's advocate, and that absence is more clearly marked and of worse effect here than abroad. The *really* unpopular, or the *really* unusual, point of view cannot get stated in pages of general circulation. And that means the absence of creative friction; for conflict is the mother of all things.

The opposition is, indeed, allowed to appear in small, obscure sheets which are devoted to nothing else. But that is of no great public service. What would be of public service would be eager and general discussion, and the perpetual presentation of argument and fact, which the public are not allowed to have.

Take such a simple point as that of Communism. It is a very living issue in our time. It is an active threat in the French commonwealth, a triumphant one in the Russian; it is a subject of immediate anxiety to every government in Europe, and though it has less place here than in any other industrial country, it does indirectly leaven a wide area of thought even here.

But to get it stated—to have said in its favour all that can be said in its favour—one must turn to small publications which are ignored by the principal newspapers and reviews. In these last you never get the Communist position fully and strongly put. You get it vaguely if violently abused—but without definitions and without concrete details; you feel that it is always there in the background, and yet you are never allowed to see it.

Let no one flatter himself that opposition can be heard because certain points of view supposedly unpopular are sometimes put in what are called "daring" or "paradoxical" essays. These are *never* true opposition. They are always either a jest or that worst form of demagogic flattery which consists in telling people what they really think but what they have not hitherto dared to say. Of true opposition in English letters we have to-day none. And English letters are badly the worse for the lack of it.

[Written in 1929 when Dean Inge, Arnold Bennett, G. K. Chesterton, and Robert Lynd were among Belloc's "colleagues in this same trade."]

II

Autumn in England

THERE is a curious fate in our treatment of days and works and landscape, of real things that we know and have present to our senses: a sort of illusion which literature has created, and print very greatly increased: it is the effect of antiquity, and therefore of the Mediterranean, on the names we give to things up here in the North.

All our tradition, our culture, is based upon that immemorial civilization which made the city state of the inland sea; and what its people experienced, what was real to them, is thrown somewhat unreally, like a coloured light, over the things immediate to ourselves.

It is so with the seasons. The ancients marked four—a brief, unpleasing winter; a long and calm but vigorous and delightful spring; a summer the full heat of which they found excessive; and an autumn which was a whole section of the year; two full months at least of vintage and of late fruits, and of a mellow, declining sun. These images they have transmitted to us; but they are here unreal; and Keats, who wrote the noblest lines upon the fall of the year, wrote them as they might have been written in Tuscany, but not as they should be to ring true of the woods between the Channel and the Midlands.

The English autumn is primarily an introduction to the vigorous but too prolonged winter of the North. It is the time when the first great gales come bowling up from the Atlantic and shake off the dead leaves; it is the time when dampness reveals all the things of the earth to us. At its very opening, for a week in one year, a fortnight in another, not more, it may be the peaceful death of summer. And it gives throughout the woodlands (which we have preserved, more diversified and better partitioned than any other people—the great trees whose presence everywhere we owe to the aristocratic history of English land), a splendour of colour which you will find nowhere else in the world. There is not one of us but will remember some vivid day when he saw under the whitish-blue of a paling sky, the great sweep of browns and reds and purples clothing a hillside as it is clothed in no other air. The hangers of South England are especially favoured in this: the beech trees of the chalk; the sweep above Petersfield; the shoulder of Box Hill which inspired Meredith.

That brief moment which we associate (wrongly, I think) with the word "autumn" in our literature and in our mind, and which we prolong in our imagination far beyond its true limits, is but an interlude. It passes quickly. The true English autumn, which is an antechamber to the English winter, begins. Our October is a loud month, and the warmish air, laden with the rains of those thousands of miles of western sea which—more than any other influence—make this island, lasts on, often to the very end of the year and beyond it. It may be fantastic to suggest, but I for my own part feel it profoundly, that those eight weeks or so (often growing to twelve) during which the English home comes into its place as a product of the English air and sky, of the early dark and the seven unfruitful months, are the segment of the year most national, and the time in which England and Englishmen are most themselves. To that English autumn of the gales on the seas and over the bare Downs belong the oldest of the national games, of the national sayings, of the habits of comradeship peculiar to the land. And for my part, when I am far from England, I do not think of my own place in the sudden, exceedingly short, miraculous bursting of the spring, nor in the rare summer days, nor in the rare snow; but in that typical weather which has built up the race; the weather under which one can run up Arun against the strong brown tide under three reefs: the weather in which from the height of Gumber one can see those living, giant clouds of ours come bowling up from the Channel and from ocean beyond.

Then it is that this our companionable earth and sky are most our friends and that we understand them best; at least so it is with me. I returned to England from an African spring, to find the summer not so different from what I had left; or from a flooded Picard February, to find the clay of the Weald like enough to the sodden fields I had left behind overseas. And the breaking of the leaves, the gathering of the birds, the call of the cuckoo in a high Pyrenean valley, has the same *timbre*, more or less, as those same good things at home.

But it is not so with the October and the November airs; and there is no home-coming like the home-coming into an English house in their windy dusk, and it is best of all when one so comes home from off the sea.

The Character of an Historical Novel

THE historical novel is a form of literary art which differs from nearly all other in this: that if it has all the excellences required of a novel but fails in its historical side, it does more harm than good.

The historical novel which is vivid, which impresses itself upon the imagination of the reader and makes him live in the scenes it describes, convinces him at the same time that the past is what the author makes it. One who in youth has thus been strongly moved by historical fiction will never completely recover from a false impression. Bad fiction—dull, uninteresting, undifferentiated stuff—which fails to impress the imagination may be as unhistorical as it likes and do no particular harm. But you have the paradox that the better the work as mere fiction the worse its effect if the history is unsound.

One cannot have a better proof of this than in the famous instance of *Ivanhoe*. Here is a book which made a whole generation live in a supposed past. The older generation with whom I talked of the thing (for I belong to that generation which, unfortunately for itself, does not sufficiently appreciate Sir Walter Scott) read this book in youth and were as convinced that they were reading true history as they would have been convinced by the evidence of their senses. The impression conveyed was so vivid that they seem to have moved in the end of the twelfth century in England and to have conversed with their fathers. And I suppose that, more than any other book, *Ivanhoe* was responsible for the extraordinary conception of the heart of the Middle Ages which you find running through most of the work of the Victorian period. The picture of society which it conveys is at least as false as the picture of modern English society conveyed by a French provincial journalist who knows no English and has never been to England. (I could put it more strongly than that, but that is putting it strongly enough.) But *Ivanhoe* has an accurate atmosphere compared with other and worse, but happily less vivid, presentations of the past.

On the other hand, a good historical novel—that rarest of rare things—is the best educational instrument imaginable. To know the past, or even a section of the past, is to add a dimension to experience. It does more to the mind even than does travel, and for the run of men who cannot evoke the life of the past through reading its chronicles, or even from any wide acquaintance with its material remains, fiction will give what is needed.

In the past generation there was perhaps one, and only one, accurate piece of historical fiction written in the English language, and that was the *Callista* of Newman. It gives the very air of Roman Africa in the last vigour of paganism. Not only is every detail accurate, but the whole atmosphere is accurate. I cannot remember whether the author had seen Barbary or not, but, at any rate, he had the genius to reproduce at once the soil and light and horizon of the North African uplands and to clothe them with the soul of the last pagan time. The feat was the more extraordinary because the author was under every temptation to misinterpret. He was dealing with a spiritual conflict in essence similar to, and yet in surroundings far removed from, that in which he himself had engaged. He had to allow for what there was in common between all oppositions to his religion, and yet not to fall into the error of making out your middle-class provincial Roman pagan a mere replica of the modern English opponent of his, Newman's, religion. At any rate, he succeeded, and we cannot say that Wiseman in a similar attempt similarly succeeded. *Fabiola* is a meaty book, full of stuff and "go." It will always make excellent reading. But those who lay it down have not lived in pagan Rome. Those who lay down *Callista* have lived in a provincial town of North Africa under the Roman domination.

To take but one test point. We moderns of the nineteenth and twentieth centuries find it very difficult to understand the universal acceptation of magic in the pagan world. Although the world went on accepting magic (now more, now less) for centuries after the pagan decline; although there was an intense recrudescence of such belief only 300 years ago and less (especially here in England), yet we seem to lack to-day every organ by which to appreciate that feeling. When we come upon magic simply taken for granted as a matter of course by the legal tribunals of the pagan Roman Empire, by the writers, by everyone (as much taken for granted as we take larceny for granted to-day), we are bewildered.

Now, if you read *Callista* you will get in a few pages (in the passage where the old witch throws a spell upon her son and he is thereby possessed of the devil) the very marrow of the matter. Never, after reading that passage, can you regard the men who take magic for granted as mere fools or as so alien to yourself as to be incomprehensible. I think one might even say that, after reading this passage, one understands why the more maleficent forms of magic were punished with death.

It is a triumph in the reconstruction of the past.

And that point leads me to the general criticism, which I believe sound, that the main test of excellence in historical fiction is this power of solving the problem of *incomprehensibles*.

The real test of success in historical study is the making understandable these things which had hitherto bewildered.

For instance, Byzantium remained highly civilized, luxurious, and immensely wealthy for several centuries, and yet that went with tides of the most wretched and debased barbarism— Scythian, German, Mongol—outside; tides which surged right up to the gates of the city.

How was that possible? Where did the revenues come from which supported that island in the midst of that sea? Or again, to most men the prolonged, minute, theological quarrels of the

Byzantine East, lasting on for more than four hundred years (exciting men's violent interest quite as much as the most acute political quarrels of modern times, raising emotions as forcible as those raised to-day by patriotism), are quite incomprehensible to-day. Most modern historians—the great Gibbon, for instance —shirked the difficulty by laughing at it. But laughing at it does not explain it.

Now, should anyone write a good historical novel resurrecting these emotions, he would do a great service to history and his fellows. Let him make his reader feel in his bones the same excitement as the very porters on the quays of Constantinople felt upon the question of whether the Blessed Virgin should be called "Theotokos" or "Theogonos." Let him write an historical novel such that, on laying it down, the reader could say: "How well I understand those emotions! I have felt them myself as I read the book!" Anyone doing that would be a successful historian and would do more good in the teaching of history and in making men understand the development of our civilization than ever Gibbon did.

That, as it seems to me, is the prime test of success in historical fiction—not only to make the past live as it actually was, but to make its inconceivable oddities conceivable. Thus, the marvellous *After London* of Jeffries, though it is not written of the dark ages in Britain (say A.D. 500–800), yet makes one understand them as can no other book.

On the contrary, the great causes of error in historical fiction, the temptations to write it wrongly, the pitfalls into which the writer tends to fall, are mainly connected with a reading of his own time into the past. It is this which slightly, though only slightly, mars the extraordinary vivid resurrections of Robert Hugh Benson. For whilst these are true in atmosphere so long as they are dealing with anything but the English country house, the moment they touch the English country house they crash into the nineteenth century. He makes your squire under Henry VIII, or his daughter Mary, become your squire under

Victoria: a deplorable lapse, and one that mars each work of that otherwise invaluable historian.

Perhaps the best historical novel of our time is *The Cloister and the Hearth*. It comes second, at any rate, to *Callista* in recovering the past, and comes before *Callista* in the vigour of the resurrection presented. There is propaganda in it—so there is in *Callista*—but it *does* present men and women going on as men and women *did* go on in the time and place with which it deals. If anything, it has the fault of being too vivid—if that be possible; too living, so that the reader, having, so to speak, conversed with and touched a generation hundreds of years ago, tends to read into them for himself the characters of to-day. But that is an error on the right side and inevitable with the best work of this kind.

Another lesser error (but a very common one, sufficiently important) which besets historical fiction is the acceptation of conventional historical falsehoods—by which I mean the acceptation by the author (who is hardly ever a man given up in the main to the reading of history) of the fictitious character imposed by the schoolmasters of his time upon the better-known names of the past. That is an error into which Robert Hugh Benson's work also falls occasionally—though rarely. For instance, in that splendid reconstruction called *By What Authority?* he gets Thomas Cromwell accurately, and very accurately also the agony of incertitude which most of the monks and nuns felt when the question of the King's Authority was put to them. In all that, it is the life of the time which rises round the reader as he reads. But when it comes to the personality of Henry, the King, a conventional schoolroom (and Oxford and Cambridge) historical falsehood intervenes and mars the picture, like a screen of coloured glass put in between the eye and the natural colours of the landscape; for we were all taught at school and university, this author amongst the rest, that Henry VIII was a powerful, dominating man, moulding others to his will and imposing his personality upon his time. That falsehood (for it is a falsehood far from the truth) was backed up by quoting every chance phrase that might support it—such phrases, for instance, as that of the shaken Wolsey (already ill and beginning to break down), when he complained so bitterly of the royal temper of his master.

Yet if there is one thing which stands out more clearly than any other when we read all that we can read of Henry VIII, and put together in due order and proportion all the evidence we have, it is that the man was essentially weak—weak under these two tests: first, that he could not control himself (which is the only form of strength properly to be called "strength"); secondly, that he was an instrument worked upon by one stronger character after another. It is perfectly clear, for instance, that the miserable business of Ann Boleyn was worked, not by Henry, who was half maddened by her calculated resistance, but by that determined Howard woman herself. It is equally clear that the policy towards Rome and towards the monasteries was not Henry's policy but Thomas Cromwell's. And so it goes on to the end. One episode after the other, right up to the disgraceful nursing of Katherine Parr, the man is under influence. It is no contradiction of this to find that he breaks out into passions of temper, against those who control him, and destroys—or attempts to destroy—them in turn. All the organization of political power was in his hands, and there was nothing to save his victims. But these outbursts were not proofs of strength but of weakness. They were the revolt of a weak character which had found itself duped again and yet again, and screamed and stamped with rage at each such new discovery. At any rate, whether you like to call this sort of nervous instability weakness or strength, it was not the *kind* of strength which the conventional historical falsehood, from motives partly patriotic, partly religious, lends to the figure of Henry VIII. The real Henry VIII is no more like that conventional figure than was the cruel, cold, fine-edged (a little mad) military genius of Henry V like the gay young portrait of convention.

These two sources of error, then, would seem to be the most serious in the writing of historical fiction—the reading of our own time back into the past and the acceptation of the conventional figures of history in the place of the real figures; and each of these errors is so difficult to escape that hardly any author has entirely escaped them.

There is, lastly, to be noted, I think, in the matter of historical fiction a certain consoling thing, which is that success in it does not seem to depend upon any great mass of reading. The artist obtains his success in this, as in so many other fields, by some strange process of intuition, integrating, from not many isolated points of knowledge, a whole combined scheme which is true and real. You have here a phenomenon like that whereby Keats, out of some few chance translations from the Greek, recovered and presented a Greek world; or like that power whereby, with hardly any experience of life, the authoress of *Wuthering Heights* wrote what is perhaps the most living book in the English language.

He who would attempt historical fiction must, of course, read something of the period upon which he would touch, but it is astonishing how little is sufficient for the man who has the right kind of genius, and how much remains quite insufficient for the man who has it not.

A converse point is well illustrated in the famous example of Flaubert's *Salammbo*. Here is the work of a man in the very first rank of those who judge, value, and use words. His *Temptation of St. Anthony* is one of the great books of the world; I shall never be tired of returning to it. The thought is a thought recurring throughout all the doubtful story of mankind: and the Thebaïd lives—upon no great reading, upon what we all know. The thing is as good as the best sculpture of that moment when the Renaissance and the Middle Ages met; the best sculpture of Brou, or of the Ambulatory of Chartres. But in *Salammbo* I think Flaubert missed his effect. He read everything that could be read. He accumulated detail. He attempted an amalgam of the guide-book or encyclopædia and the vision, and he fell heavily between them.

You do not get the resurrection of the past by a long string of technical phrases. You get it by the "eye-opener," the sudden statement. You get it, for instance, in Joinville, when the people are coming out from Mass and one of them picks up the king's cloak and compares the stuff with his own. You get it when you hear of the Germans in South Italy ridiculing the Normans for being "dwarfs." You get it when you find the Venerable Bede counting English dates by the reigns of emperors in Constantinople. In other words, you get it in history exactly as you get it in contemporary travel—one phrase illuminates in a flash. The Frenchman reading the English phrase, "It isn't cricket," and getting to understand it, would know more about England than if he were word perfect on all the main institutions of England, including the comic labyrinth of our titles.

And I will conclude by saying that we have here a parallel in historical fiction to the writing of history itself.

The difference between the good and bad historian is not so much the difference between a wide, regular, well-ordered and a narrow, irregular, and ill-ordered reading of record. It lies much more in the two qualities of proportion and imagination. Two men, for instance, may sit down to write as historians the events of an ancient battle. The one, by the use of a strong memory applied to industrious reading, may make himself acquainted with a thousand points where his rival is acquainted with ten. But the space of each is limited, and even if each had an unlimited canvas on which to paint, the truth of the result would still depend upon proportion—upon the discovery of the essential movements and the essential moments in the action; and upon imagination, the power of seeing the thing as it was; landscape, the weather, the gestures and the faces of the men; yes, and their thoughts within.

IV

On Megalomania

WHETHER it be moral or immoral I know not, but I find a certain pleasure in the extravagances of human life, and most of all in what is absurdly called to-day "megalomania." Our fathers called it by a simpler name, and our cousins (as we are pleased to style them) have discovered one simpler still—for they call it "swelled head."

And yet, when I come to think of it, the swelled head is not a characteristic of megalomania. There is in the swelled head a sort of self-centred appetite. The fellow who suffers from it is thinking all the time of himself—not of his surroundings. He is angry if he is belittled. He is sure that he writes great verse when as a fact he writes doggerel. He is offended when people treat him as of no importance in the commonwealth, though indeed he be of none.

But my darling the megalomaniac is not built on these lines. He considers externals, and hardly anything else. What is amiable about the megalomaniac is also amiable about the child. He lives in a fancy world of his own making, which is real to him; and if he desires to have castles and retainers and courtiers of all sorts about him, it is not because he is proud, it is because such adjuncts are picturesque. They inflate him, but not with vanity; rather with colour, and movement, and life. Moreover, having made his fiction, he dare not depart from it.

I knew one such many years ago, who was a public man, and we were friends more or less. We were not intimate friends, but I got on with him, and we used to discuss Parliament and its pomposities (which interested him enormously and bored me to tears). Now, this good fellow would often invite people to his country-seat in a distant part of this island. He would do so in a solemn fashion, made up both of ritual and of kindness. He hated to make his acquaintances feel inferior. He did not disdain to place his right hand upon their left shoulder, and when he talked of his rank and of his traditions it was always in a sidelong fashion and with a lowered voice.

"If you come and call on us—and I do so hope you will do so—remember that we do not keep up the main drive to the house any longer. The plain truth is, we cannot afford it. It is rather more than a mile from the West Lodge to the Inigo Jones portico, and we have had to let it go down to grass. People turn in there because there is still a bit of gravel dating from my grandfather's time, but it is difficult. If there has been any rain you might get stuck. Go right round to the *back* of the park if you don't mind, and in by the lower lodge, the one we call 'Bateman's.' It is only half a mile from there to the house, and we have kept it up. You will find the old place half shut up—you know, we are not what we were—but we'll give you a welcome, I think. . . ."

And having said these things, he would silently and sadly slouch away.

In this fashion my acquaintance impressed very great numbers of those poor people who come up to London and wait patiently to pester politicians under the impression that politicians can help them. And not a few did he impress even of the richer people, for these also are gullible. He impressed me, who was neither of one nor of the other.

I never knew anyone who went to that noble but decayed house of his, whether by the Gate of Horn or by the Gate of Ivory, whether by the Sad Gate of Truth or by the Happy Gate of Dreams, whether by the Upper or the Lower Drive. But this I know: that when he came to die, it turned out all too truly that a widowed mother, scraping every penny to put him into public life, had died where he himself also lived: in a semi-detached brick villa outside a manufacturing town. And in front of it there were two monkey trees.

Then, also I have known fifteen separate men who were each

responsible for the Great War, and I cannot tell you how many more who were each responsible for the peace. I have known those men who prophesied the Armistice to the month, day, and hour: they told me so immediately after.

It is now some years since a man appeared in my neighbourhood, in a town about twenty miles from my house, who had been many years ago not undistinguished in English Letters, but had fallen upon evil days. He said to a friend of mine and to me, "I have come down here without my man. He will be following in a few days. I am afraid I have got no one to cook for me. May I come in and have meals with you?" He came in and had meals. He had no man. He was lodged in a garret. He died humbly enough, for it is difficult to die in any other fashion. But almost to the end he kept up this pretence of past greatness. Well, I suppose he was none the worse for it.

They are quite different from the ambitious, this sort of men. They are often confused with them because each kind is worrying about grandeur—or his ideas of grandeur. But they are opposite in their way of taking grandeur. For the ambitious man strikes for it and makes it his goal. The megalomaniac has it already. The ambitious man is never satisfied. There is always some greater thing ahead which he does not reach. But the megalomaniac is satisfied from the beginning and is happy all the time.

I knew a man once who wanted to be mayor of a provincial town where I was lecturing. He had restless bright eyes, and he courted everyone he met. He became mayor. After that, he wanted a knighthood. He got a knighthood. After that it would seem there was nothing left but to repose in glory, for he had reached the summit of human affairs. Yet when I visited him in old age, it was not so. He was still restless, his eyes were still bright, he still desired some further greatness; what, I could not imagine. But after his death I was told that he had ardently desired an O.B.E.

Now, in that man's very house and at his very table I used to meet another, dark-haired, purposeful, but solid and serenely happy. He greeted me always as a colleague in letters. He told me he confined himself to verse, and every time I saw him he would give me the latest figures of his sales. One little fragrant volume had sold 40,000. Another he was bringing out shortly had already been subscribed by the booksellers to bigger figures than that. Ought he to try fiction? I strongly advised it. Was a thirty per cent. royalty fair? I thought it excellent. Was an advance of £500 on a projected anthology (payable on signing contract) sufficient? I told him that, as anthologies go, it was ample.

From such descriptions he ceased not until I lost sight of him: and lately I have heard that he, too, is dead. He was happy to the end. He never published . . . but he was one of England's great bards by the only test that counts, which is the judgment of the secure mind within. He was wholly free of the base bonds, the chains of human respect, dependence on the petty praise of men. He wrote, he published, he was acclaimed in Paradise.

I would rather be the second man than the first, and that for several reasons. First, I don't like municipal duties; secondly, I doubt if one can ever get (in external reality and outside the mind) what one wants; thirdly, I wouldn't mind fame as a poet; and fourthly, I hate writing. But all that is no one else's business, so I will put it aside, but in closing, ask you this: Have you ever found in history or experience an ambitious man who found happiness or a megalomaniac who missed it?

V

The Horseman of Varennes

[This sketch reproduces an historical episode, as from the imagined recollection of the principal agent.]

IN the town of Mâcon in France on the Burgundian river Saône there still lived in 1824 an elderly gentleman called Meyer. He was in his sixty-first year. No one knew exactly where he had come from, save that his papers were all in order and that he had until a few years before lived abroad. The name Meyer, German in form, was not unknown in that part of the country. No one questioned him. He lived in retirement on some small income, and was popular enough within the little circle of his acquaintance. He was a small man, still alert and vigorous, lean and taut, his eyes bright and moving rapidly like those of a bird, and his thin nose was like the beak of a bird, aquiline. There came one night of that year '24 three younger men of various ages, one of them only just past his boyhood, the other two in the thirties and forties, relatives of the lad whom they had brought with them.

The three had come to pass the evening with Meyer at his invitation. There was wine ready for them on the table. When they had greeted their host and he them, he stood up suddenly, even abruptly for a man of such years, and addressed them like one making a speech.

"I have asked you to come round and drink wine with me to-night, my friends," he said, "in order to carry out a certain purpose of mine which you will understand in a moment. I have chosen you because, after now some years of acquaintance with your characters, I am confident that I can entrust you with my story, and I have asked your young relative to come with you because I think it well that one of his generation should be witness to what I have to tell, and carry it on till the passions of our time shall have been forgotten.

"You will have heard from your elders much about that famous night, Midsummer's Night of '91? You were told how King Louis, the present King's brother, was stopped during his flight from Paris with his wife and children in the town of Varennes, just on the far side of the Argonne hills and their deep forest."

"Yes," said the oldest of the three guests, "I can even remember the news coming to our house and the excitement. I was a child at the time, but I shall never forget the impression it made on me. My father talked of it for weeks. All the circumstances were so striking. It was a matter of minutes and of yards. Another five minutes, another quarter mile, and they would have been across the bridge and safe within the outposts of the army. And then its coming as it did, at dead of night, and all that turned upon it!"

Meyer still stood before them, watching the speaker keenly and nodding assent at each point; but he did not yet speak, and after a pause the second guest put in his word.

"You are right. Everything turned upon it. If the King had got away to the army, the army would have marched on Paris. That would have been the end of the great change."

Meyer still stood silent, watching them keenly. He again nodded his agreement. Then he spoke.

"I have asked you here to-night because I want to tell you in detail, as no other man now living can, what happened in that dark and famous hour. You all of you remember the name of the man who did the trick? The man who intercepted the carriage of the fugitives and stopped it in the nick of time?"

"Oh yes, we all know that. This youngster here knows it best of all, for he is fresh from school."

The young man piped up: "It was Drouet. The man was called Drouet. He was the son of the postmaster at Ste. Menehould on the other side of the hills."

"That's it! That's it!" said little, active, grizzled, elderly Meyer, leaning over him. "That's it. Drouet was the name. . . . Well, *I am Drouet*!"

He spoke those words with the sort of triumph men use when they know they can affirm an amazing thing. He put forth his hand authoritatively to check any interruption. "I am Drouet," he repeated. "You may guess that after King Louis XVI was put to death I was marked for Royalist vengeance. After Napoleon's fall and the return of the monarchy I fled beyond the Rhine. I lived in exile some years, and then crept back here under this false name to die in peace; but before I die I will bear witness to the part I played. I am determined that exact knowledge of all that happened shall not perish or be set down wrongly, for on the mighty doings of those years there are a hundred stories. I alone can tell you exactly what passed. I have kept silent upon it during all those years of exile, and now I relate it to you of set purpose. Listen to my story.

"I was coming in to the market square of Ste. Menehould with my scythe over my shoulder at the end of that summer's day, June 21st, 1791. I had been mowing the last of the grass in my father's fields. As I thus came into the market-place the sun, which had been hidden in high clouds all day, appeared just as it was setting in the west. A few minutes later but while it was still broad daylight, a cabriolet came in at a good pace piloting a very large and heavy private coach, yellow in colour, with green blinds and topped with a mass of luggage. This equipage came in by the Châlons road. The horses were in foam, for they had been pressed. The postilions set foot to ground, the unharnessing began, and I told my men to get the relay horses out to take the travellers on to the next stage, which was Clermont, beyond the woods, on the high-road to Metz.

"There had been rumours about all day. Some of the royal cavalry, German mercenaries, had been seen in the fields to the north, first riding westward as though making for some point on the Châlons road, then back eastward through the forest. A man of my trade gives little credit to rumours. We hear too many of them in the posting-houses. All the world knew of the great quarrel that was being worked out in Paris, and half the world expected that the king would fly. As for me, I worried less than most. I had been a soldier in my time. I was as good a patriot as any other man, but I would do nothing rash.

"Just as the relay horses were harnessed and the coach with its light forerunner was starting out again, it being now dusk, the green blind of the near side of the coach went up and a man looked out as though to take a breath of air in the cool of that midsummer evening. Even as his face appeared, a girl among those who had gathered cried out shrilly, 'It is the King!'

"Some looked round, some murmured, but the cabriolet started off smartly and the big coach behind it. I called out to my men not to kill their cattle on the steep hill-sides of the Argonne, for there was a deep valley between Ste. Menehould and Clermont, the next stage.

"It was after the coach was well out of the town that the hubbub began. Many began to swear that it was the King and Queen. They had noticed how the captain of the troop billeted in the town had respectfully saluted the face at the window. They were so convinced that I was inclined to agree. The town council was called. My father was the most prominent man upon it. I was summoned and said at last that I thought I had recognized the travellers. It *might* be they. Those about the board became more and more certain. Someone pulled out a bank-note on which was printed a picture of the King's face, and men crowded round, peering over each other's shoulders, saying: 'Yes, it was they!' They recognized the royal face printed on the note. Later it was said that I started this, but indeed the King had been recognized even as far back as Châlons, only men had held their tongues.

"As the excitement grew the council took swift decisions. They arrested the captain of the billeted troop; they nominated me to ride after the fugitives at full speed and warn the countryside.

"I did as I was told. The choice was a wise one, for I was a good rider and had done my seven years in the dragoons. I took with me Guillaume, an ex-dragoon like myself. We saddled the last two horses remaining in the stables, and we were off up the Clermont road, which is the main road to Metz. We took it for granted that the King—if it *was* the King—would be taking refuge with the garrison of Metz; but we were wrong, and the error proved to be our opportunity.

"It was already one hour since the coach had rolled away. The King had that hour's start of us! We galloped on through the night. About a mile before the Clermont post we crossed our men coming back with the horses after the relay. They told us great news. At Clermont the royal coach had left the Metz road and turned off sharp to the left, to the north, making for Varennes.

"You will see how it was, the big coach had only about ten miles to go before it would reach the main outposts of the army line just beyond Varennes town—nothing like as far as Metz. Our chances of getting the King were far greater, and, most decisive point of all, *we might now intercept him and cut off his flight*. To pursue along the paved high-road, merely following the fugitives, might have been fruitless. We did not know how far out from Metz the army might not have thrown forward patrols, and, at any rate, to try and halt postilions whom you are with difficulty catching up is one thing—to make them halt by getting in front of them is another. This is what we now had a chance of doing. We could avoid the main road, cut off the elbow by going through the woods and so getting ahead of our quarry. We could only do it by the very best of luck. No check in the dark at a fallen tree-trunk or a boggy patch of soil and our horses holding out in spite of the hard going. But it was a chance —and to go on to Clermont and follow along the road would be longer, and there might be patrols out on the way.

"I had to make up my mind at once. I would cut off the corner, I and my companion; by galloping through the forest and getting all we could out of our mounts, it might be just barely possible to reach Varennes thus through the wood in time before the coach should get in. But the odds were against us.

"I heard the distant clock at Clermont strike ten as Guillaume and I plunged uphill over the hard clay to the green ride that follows the ridge through the trees. Once there, we galloped on, hell for leather, taking all the risks of those miles in the deep darkness, until we saw the branch lane which goes off down the slope to the right and a few lights still shining in the windows of Varennes town. We did not pause on that rough descent; luckily there was no stumble. We only drew rein when we reached the main street where the high-road comes in. There we halted, but we heard nothing. For my part I thought we might have got in too late, but not two minutes later Guillaume said that he heard the distant sound of wheels and horses. I knew at once what to do. We found a heavy furniture-van near the river-side and pushed it forward till it blocked the bridge. We primed our pistols and went up across the square. Even as we went we heard eleven striking from the town clock of Varennes.

"At the top of the square, where the main road comes in, it runs through an archway. By that archway we stood all ready for them. When the headlights suddenly glared upon us, when first the cabriolet and then the coach came thundering under the vault, I leapt forward, seized the reins of the leaders and threw them back on their haunches, shouting to the postilions to halt and dismount.

"There was a clamour within the carriages, a woman's voice begging to be let through, for they were in haste; but it was too late. People were running up from all sides, many of them with arms. There was no chance of rescue now, nor did any of the troops beyond the bridge appear. Our purpose was accomplished and our ride was done."

On the Selection of Books

IT is astonishing what a herd of people nowadays want to be told what to read. It has become a disease, spreading throughout the mass. I recoil from it with horror. Surely to goodness a man knows his own taste, and surely to gracious goodness a woman knows hers! But it would seem to have come to books as it has long since come to wine, to pictures, to architecture, to furniture, to common morals, and even to the plain business of thinking and reasoning, that the paralysis of our time has destroyed all power of selection.

It is now a generation since a banker told the world what were the hundred best books in his, the banker's judgment. What service this could be to anyone I cannot imagine. Why a hundred, and how "best"? And for that matter, what are the limits of "a book" in this sense? Is the Bible a book? Or the Book of Mormon (which I have yet to read, though I talked about it a good deal in Salt Lake City forty years ago with an elderly, long-bearded, saturnine man, who is now, I hope, receiving his reward)? Are the works, certain and doubtful, of William Shakespeare a book? Is the larger Larousse, in twenty-odd fat volumes of close print, four columns a page, a book?

And again, what does such a list presuppose? Are you engaged in forgetting the world, or in learning it, or in producing a happy mood, or tickling yourself with horror, panic, cruelty, dirt, despair, and the general devilment? What are you after, you and your hundred best books. . . . Forsooth?

And again I say Forsooth!

However, since there is this present craze for catching hold of other people's hands to help the blind through their darkness, I shall be happy to oblige with a set of simple rules which are my own for the selection of books. If you ask me what purpose that can serve, if you tell me roughly that my private habits in this private matter concern no one but myself, I answer that I abound in your sense, that I agree with you from mascot to luggage carrier and from the sliding roof to the underside of the four tyres. I am wholly of your mind; for I would not myself take anybody else's advice in the matter, anyhow, and least of all would I advise anyone to take my own—for reasons which will shortly be apparent. But as hardly a day passes without my getting a letter on these lines of inanity, as dozens of the things called "symposiums" are swept up together daily on those same fatuous lines, why, here goes! You do not want to know on what principles I would select books? I will tell you on what principles I select books.

First, a selection means elimination. Now, there are published in England to-day (without making mention of the lesser breeds without the law in France, Germany, Holland, Belgium, Italy, and Spain, the two Americas, China, Africa, and the Vatican State) three hundred and twenty-four point six seven two recurring books (upon the average) every hour. Many of these are paid for, I am glad to say, through the silly vanity of their authors. On nearly all the others the publishers lose; but they make so much on the odd few that happen (no mortal can tell you why) to take with the public, that they well recover their losses in the gamble and are able to build those great palaces which everywhere delight the eye of us poor scribblers. (How often, wandering over the hills of England, have I seen from afar off a noble mansion in the Corinthian manner, and have asked a passing swain, "Surely that is the seat of the Marquis of Carabas?" who has replied, "Why, no, sir. It is where Mr. Barabbas, the publisher, lives." And I have gone away with a mist of tears before my eyes!)

Well, then, if books are pouring out at this rate, the first and main principle of selection is not to meddle with them at all if you can help it. Keep out of their way. Blow your horn vigorously and thread your way through the flock till you can get a clear road on the far side, and then buzz off.

There is, however, a frailty in man which compels him, in spite of himself, to read when once he has learnt to read, just as he is compelled to smoke when once he has broken himself in, with much nausea, through his teens, to the beastly habit of smoking. In spite of yourself you will find yourself picking up books, opening them at random and glancing at a line or two of the stodge within.

It is here that my second principle comes in. If, in such picking and choosing of a few words, you find a glimmer of sense, of humour, or of information, account yourself a discoverer and have a stab at the thing. It will probably prove not worth your while; the first page will be quite enough to tell you. But if it turns out just tolerable, why, then, supposing you have nothing else to do, attempt to read it. You need not read it through.

My third principle in the choice of books is to go by externals: binding and title, but especially print and paper. Even a book worth reading, even one of the great classics (such as *The Tale of a Tub*), is the more readable in strong, clear, square type on proper thick paper and with reasonable margins. It is on this account that the wise, when they desire to taste a library, prefer books printed in the later eighteenth century.

My fourth principle is this: let the book you reluctantly persuade yourself to read be in your native language, unless, indeed, it be in Greek or Latin. One is sure to under-estimate or over-estimate a book in a modern foreign language and, what is worse, the reading of books in foreign languages may lead one into accepting the opinions of others and that morass of literary snobbery in which a million drown every season.

You may now think that I have done; but I have not, for I propose to conclude by contradicting myself. There *is* one kind of book that I *do* ferret out with joy, and I beg you all to copy my example. There *is* one kind of book for which I keep a sharp look-out and which I have come to recognize at a glance, instinctively, among a thousand titles in a catalogue of no matter what small print, or in the density of no matter what underwood of reviews—and that is the book written by an opponent: the book written in defence of what I hate.

The morsel is the more delicious if it be academic; it can be received the more joyfully in proportion as it is ill written, dull, unreadable, and absurd. Fasten upon it with the twenty claws of your soul. Check the references. Blue-pencil the misprints. Score the anomalies, the great gaps in knowledge, the inconsistencies. It is savoury meat. It nourishes a man. O Combat! Universal Genetrix and Breeder of all things that be, how can I sufficiently praise you, even in this vapid field of letters? You are best in the perilous chances of Cythera, or in chase, or under sail, or in physical triumphs of the body, or in arms, but you are not to be despised even here in the realm of printer's ink! Holy Writ, which is full of so many good things, confirms me, and gives me the right phrase with which to set a seal to my judgment. For of its many rhetorical optative phrases (which long for the wings of a dove, for peace, for justice and, in exile, for the native land), none strikes a stronger chord in the human heart than that profound, that major cry, "Oh, that mine enemy had written a book!" I am glad to say he sometimes has.

VII

On Cooking

TEN years ago I read, on the deck of a tramp steamer which was taking me for eight shillings from Coruña to Santander, a translation of the learned but fanatical Mommsen's history of Rome. In that work I came upon a sentence in which the twisted author ascribed the decline of States to good cooking. That is your Teutonic School of History all over! "What I do well is the mark of strength. What I do badly is the mark of weakness. That is why I am so strong and foreigners so contemptible." It is the mood which breeds defeat, as the unfortunate compatriots of Mommsen now know.

Anyhow, the falsity of the sentence stuck in my mind, and ever since then I have considered the vast advantage to the State of Good Cooking and the disasters that attend neglect of the kitchen: defeat in the field, famine, despair.

So when I got Lady Jekyll's *Kitchen Essays* the other day I determined both that I would write upon it and that I would not ask the leave of the editor to review it. I cannot review save upon one or two small departments where I have worked up an amount of detailed material. I will review you a book upon the Donation of Constantine or upon the Second Council of Nicaea, for I have read the original documents that are to be read upon these two things. And I shall be pretty sure, beforehand, of a feast of criticism: for such books are generally charlatan anti-Christian stuff. But I will not review a book on cookery, because I cannot cook. And as for reviewing a book of fiction (or what is called fiction nowadays, which is the boring discussion of why insignificant people do insignificant and usually dirty things), I would no more do that than I would walk ten miles blindfold on a moonless night through the December rain for nothing. But though I cannot review, I was determined to write upon this matter of cooking because it is of such high importance and yet so scurvily treated.

Lady Jekyll's book is just what ought to have been done I know not how often before, and what has not been done. I mean a description of cookery by the blank for the blank. I put the word "blank" because almost any word I should use to fill up that blank would be abused. If I should say "by the cultured for the cultured," people would say that "culture" was a horrid word, or that it meant nothing, or that it was priggish. If I said "by the educated for the educated," they would say the word was false and vague, and if I said "gentlefolk" or "gentry," or anything of that kind, they would let the dogs loose. But, anyhow, my point is that cooking is one of those things which ought to be written about by the blank for the blank—and never are. Your classical cookery books (and there are a great deal too many of them) are not written for the person who has to eat the stuff; yet, after all, he or she ought first to be considered.

My next point is much more important. It is this: Your ordinary cookery book (and it is true of the good French cookery books quite as much as of the English) takes a mass of things for granted. It is the bad mark of all technical books that they do that. Indeed, the publishers of Lady Jekyll's book have hinted at something of the sort in their notice of it. For we are told there that the buyer must have some knowledge of cooking and of cooking terms before he can use it. I don't agree. The great value of the book, to me, a layman, lies in its telling me in plain terms how to carry on. Of course the reader must have some knowledge. He must know what is meant by "salt" and by a "calf's foot," and so on, but the curse attaching to most cookery books and all "How to do it" books is the curse of bringing in technical terms which are *just beyond the boundary* where ordinary culture stops. We all know what that means. We get it in books on any science you may like to name, and it mars them all.

For instance, if I am explaining a problem in navigation to an

average educated man, I should not explain the words "equator,"
"pole," "latitude," "longitude," because your educated man
knows what these words mean; but I should explain the term
"great-circle sailing," simple as it is, because it is just over the
margin of technicality.

Or again, I should, in talking of the Angevin glory in England
to a man of average education, say it "began a hundred years
or so after the Battle of Hastings," for every man of average
education knows the date of Hastings, and every man of average
education would be rightly insulted if you called it by the absurd
name of Senlac. But I should not, to a man of average education,
say "it began about the time of the Constitutions of Clarendon,"
because a man of average education does not know the date of
the Constitutions of Clarendon.

It is so with cooking. Tell a reader that he must use stock in
such an amount and he knows what you mean. Tell him that he
must "Echaudez pour un instant, puis eteignez avec deux doigts
de Marinade en Mouvette," and he does not know what you
mean. I think this principle can be developed pretty far. I notice
that half-educated people (excuse me the term) are passionately
fond of involving their readers in technicalities, but the mark of
your cultivated man is that he knows exactly where men of his
own culture stand in a matter.

My third point, which is a great deal more important than my
second, is that Lady Jekyll's book tells me in each case what I
may irreverently call "the trick." There is no one who has
cooked but has discovered that each particular dish depends for
its rightness upon some little point which he is never told. It is
not only so of cooking: it is so of splicing a rope; of painting a
surface of wood; of mixing mortar; of almost anything you
like to name among the immemorial human arts. There is one
little point on which everything turns, and that is exactly the
point left out. Now, here I find it told, and I am grateful in
proportion to my need. For instance (I purposely quote not
from the book but from my own experience), what is the art in

the making of bouillon? What is the trick which makes all the difference? You may have the most exact ingredients, you may put in just the right amount of salt, and you may take all the trouble in life, but you will make the most abominable bouillon unless you boil the meat very smartly indeed for some twenty minutes, and *then*, and not *till* then, let it simmer quite slowly for hours and hours. Let it simmer from the beginning and you have a horror. Boil it all along and you have a sort of watery stuff.

Or again, why not tell people that if you put the paper of meringues on metal you fail, while if you put it on wood you succeed?

Or again, why not tell people that in the sauce called Neuburg for a lobster, somewhat too little sherry is tolerable but too much ruins it: and why not tell them the exact amount for two eggs?

Or again, why not tell people, in so simple a matter as boiling an egg, that when you have the water boiling the boiling generally stops after you put the egg in, and that therefore you must not count the time from the moment you put the egg in, but from the moment you see the water boiling again?

One might go on quoting such cases for ever. The glory of a good cookery book is that it tells you these things. In fact, one might do worse than issue a little cookery book after the fashion of a book called *Don't*, which was famous half a lifetime ago, and which told people how to behave among the very rich. It said, among other things, if I remember right, "Don't throw yourself too much upon your hostess." (But that may be a lapse of memory on my part. I may be thinking of an etiquette book which we found in a man's room at Balliol, when I was young —he was a North-country man—and which we illustrated from cover to cover.) For the art of cooking really lies in these don'ts. It is the detail which people go wrong on, it is one particular "don't" which spoils a dish; and a spoiled dish might as well not be cooked at all.

If I ever write a cookery book I shall begin by telling my readers that the best meal in the world is bread, salt, wine, and an onion (which need no cooking), and I shall go on to talk of other things than cooking, for I confess to irrelevance. And, after all, what does it matter? Writing is a poor trade, but cooking is sacred. Any fool can write, but to cook . . .

VIII

On Walking

S o long as man does not bother about what he is or whence he came or whither he is going, the whole thing seems as simple as the verb "to be"; and you may say that the moment he does begin thinking about what he is (which is more than thinking that he is) and whence he came and whither he is going, he gets on to a lot of roads that lead nowhere, and that spread like the fingers of a hand or the sticks of a fan; so that if he pursues two or more of them he soon gets beyond his straddle, and if he pursues only one he gets farther and farther from the rest of all knowledge as he proceeds. You may say that and it will be true. But there is one kind of knowledge a man does get when he thinks about what he is, whence he came and whither he is going, which is this: that it is the only important question he can ask himself.

Now, the moment a man begins asking himself those questions (and all men begin at some time or another if you give them rope enough), man finds himself a very puzzling fellow. There was a school—it can hardly be called a school of philosophy—and it is now as dead as mutton, but anyhow there *was* a school which explained the business in the very simple method known to the learned as tautology—that is, saying the same thing over and over again. For just as the woman in Molière was dumb because she was affected with the quality of dumbness, so man, according to this school, did all the extraordinary things he does do because he had developed in that way. They took in a lot of people while they were alive (I believe a few of the very old ones still survive), they took in nobody more than themselves; but they have not taken in any of the younger generation. We who come after these scientists continue to ask ourselves the old question, and if there is no finding of an answer to it, so much the worse; for asking it, every instinct of our nature tells us, is the proper curiosity of man.

Of the great many things which man does which he should not do or need not do, if he were wholly explained by the verb "to be," you may count walking. Of course, if you build up a long series of guesses as to the steps by which he learnt to walk, and call *that* an explanation, there is no more to be said. It is as though I were to ask you why Mr. Smith went to Liverpool, and you were to answer by giving me a list of all the stations between Euston and Lime Street in their exact order. At least that is what it would be like if your guesses were accurate, not only in their statement, but also in their proportion and also in their order. It is millions to one that your guesses are nothing of the kind. But even granted by a miracle that you have got them all quite right (which is more than the wildest fanatic would grant to the dearest of his geologians), it tells me nothing.

What on earth persuaded the animal to go on like that? Or was it nothing on earth but something in heaven?

Just watch a man walking, if he is a proper man, and see the business of it: how he expresses his pride, or his determination, or his tenacity, or his curiosity, or perhaps his very purpose in his stride! Well, all that business of walking that you are looking at is a piece of extraordinarily skilful trick-acting, such that were the animal not known to do it you would swear he could never be trained to it by any process, however lengthy, or however minute, or however strict. This is what happens when a man walks: first of all he is in stable equilibrium, though the arc of stability is minute. If he stands with his feet well apart, his centre of gravity (which is about half-way up him or a little more) may oscillate within an arc of about five degrees on either side of stability and tend to return to rest. But if it oscillates beyond that five degrees or so, the stability of his equilibrium is lost and down he comes. Men have been known to sleep standing up without a support, especially on military service, which is the most fatiguing thing in the world; but it is extremely rare, and you may say of a man so standing, even with his feet well spread, that he is already doing a fine athletic feat.

But wait a moment: he desires to go, to proceed, to reach a distant point, and instead of going on all fours, where equilibrium would indeed be stable, what does he do? He deliberately lifts one of his supports off the ground, and sends his equilibrium to the devil; at the same time he leans a little forward so as to make himself fall towards the object he desires to attain. You do not know that he does this, but that is because you are a man and your ignorance of it is like the ignorance in which so many really healthy people stand to religion, or the ignorance of a child who thinks his family established for ever in comfort, wealth, and security. What you really do, man, when you want to get to that distant place (and let this be a parable of all adventure and of all desire) is to take an enormous risk, the risk of coming down bang and breaking something: you lift one foot off the ground, and, as though that were not enough, you deliberately throw your centre of gravity forward so that you begin to fall.

That is the first act of the comedy.

The second act is that you check your fall by bringing the foot which you had swung into the air down upon the ground again.

That you would say was enough of a bout. Slide the other foot up, take a rest, get your breath again and glory in your feat. But not a bit of it! The moment you have got that loose foot of yours firm on the earth, you use the impetus of your first tumble to begin another one. You get your centre of gravity by the momentum of your going well forward of the foot that has found the ground, you lift the other foot without a care, you let it swing in the fashion of a pendulum, and you check your second fall in the same manner as you checked your first; and even after that second clever little success you do not bring your feet both firmly to the ground to recover yourself before the next venture: you go on with the business, get your centre of gravity forward of the foot that is now on the ground, swinging the other beyond it like a pendulum, stopping your third catastrophe, and so on; and you have come to do all this so that you think it the most natural thing in the world!

Not only do you manage to do it but you can do it in a thousand ways, as a really clever acrobat will astonish his audience not only by walking on the tight-rope but by eating his dinner on it. You can walk quickly or slowly, or look over your shoulder as you walk, or shoot fairly accurately as you walk; you can saunter, you can force your pace, you can turn which way you will. You certainly did not teach yourself to accomplish this marvel, nor did your nurse. There was a spirit within you that taught you and that brought you out; and as it is with walking, so it is with speech, and so at last with humour and with irony, and with affection, and with the sense of colour and of form, and even with honour, and at last with prayer.

By all this you may see that man is very remarkable, and this should make you humble, not proud; for you have been designed in spite of yourself for some astonishing fate, of which these mortal extravagances so accurately seized and so well moulded you to your being, are but the symbols.

Walking, like talking (which rhymes with it, I am glad to say), being so natural a thing to man, so varied and so unthought about, is necessarily not only among his chief occupations but among his most entertaining subjects of commonplace and of exercise.

Thus to walk without an object is an intense burden, as it is to talk without an object. To walk because it is good for you warps the soul, just as it warps the soul for a man to talk for hire or because he thinks it his duty. On the other hand, walking with an object brings out all that there is in a man, just as talking with an object does. And those who understand the human body, when they confine themselves to what they know and are therefore legitimately interesting, tell us this very interesting thing which experience proves to be true: that walking, of every form of exercise, is the most general and the most complete, and that while a man may be endangered by riding a horse or by running or swimming, or while a man may easily exaggerate any violent movement, walking will always be to his benefit—that is, of course, so long as he does not warp his soul by the detestable habit of walking for no object but exercise. For it has been so arranged that the moment we begin any minor and terrestrial thing as an object in itself, or with merely the furtherance of some other material thing, we hurt the inward part of us that governs all. But walk for glory or for adventure, or to see new sights, or to pay a bill or to escape the same, and you will very soon find how consonant is walking with your whole being. The chief proof of this (and how many men have tried it, and in how many books does not that truth shine out!) is the way in which a man walking becomes the cousin or the brother of everything around.

If you will look back upon your life and consider what landscapes remain fixed in your memory, some perhaps you will discover to have struck you at the end of long rides or after you have been driven for hours, dragged by an animal or a machine. But much the most of these visions have come to you when you were performing that little miracle with a description of which I began this: and what is more, the visions that you get when you are walking merge pleasantly into each other. Some are greater, some lesser, and they make a continuous whole. The great moments are led up to and are fittingly framed.

There is no time or weather, in England at least, in which a man walking does not feel this cousinship with everything around. There are weathers that are intolerable if you are doing anything else but walking: if you are crouching still against a storm or if you are driving against it; or if you are riding in extreme cold; or if you are running too quickly in extreme heat; but it is not so with walking. You may walk by night or by day, in summer or in winter, in fair weather or in foul, in calm or in a gale, and in every case you are doing something native to yourself and going the best way you could go. All men have felt this.

Walking, also from this same natural quality which it has, introduces particular sights to you in their right proportion. A man gets into his motor-car, or more likely into somebody else's, and covers a great many miles in a very few hours. And what remains to him at the end of it, when he looks closely into the pictures of his mind, is a curious and unsatisfactory thing: there are patches of blurred nothingness like an uneasy sleep, one or two intense pieces of impression, disconnected, violently vivid and mad, a red cloak, a shining streak of water, and more particularly a point of danger. In all that ribbon of sights, each either much too lightly or much too heavily impressed, he is lucky if there is one great view which for one moment he seized and retained from a height as he whirled along. The whole record is like a bit of dry-point that has been done by a hand not sure of itself upon a plate that trembled—now jagged chiselling bit into the metal; now blurred or hardly impressed it at all: only in some rare moment of self-possession or of comparative repose did the hand do what it willed and transfer its power.

You may say that, riding upon a horse, one has a better chance. That is true, but, after all, one is busy riding. Look back upon the very many times that you have ridden, and though you will remember many things, you will not remember them in that calm and perfect order in which they presented themselves to you when you were afoot. As for a man running, if it be for any distance, the effort is so unnatural as to concentrate upon himself all a man's powers, and he is almost blind to exterior things. Men at the end of such efforts are actually and physically blind; they fall helpless.

Then there is the way of looking at the world which rich men imagine they can purchase with money when they build a great house looking over some view—but it is not in the same street with walking! You see the sight nine times out of ten when you are ill attuned to it, when your blood is slow and unmoved, and when the machine is not going. When you are walking, the machine is always going, and every sense in you is doing what it should with the right emphasis and in due discipline to make a perfect record of all that is about.

Consider how a man walking approaches a little town; he sees it a long way off upon a hill; he sees its unity, he has time to think about it a great deal. Next it is hidden from him by a wood or it is screened by a roll of land. He tops this and sees the little town again, now much nearer, and he thinks more particularly of its houses, of the way in which they stand, and of what has passed in them. The sky, especially if it has large white clouds in it and is for the rest sunlit and blue, makes something against which he can see the little town and gives it life. Then he is at the outskirts, and he does not suddenly occupy it with a clamour or a rush, nor does he merely contemplate it, like a man from a window, unmoving. He enters in. He passes, healthily wearied, human doors and signs; he can note all the names of the people and the trade at which they work; he has time to see their faces. The square broadens before him, or the market-place, and so very naturally and rightly he comes to his inn, and he has fulfilled one of the great ends of man.

Lord, how tempted one is here to make a list of those monsters who are the enemies of inns!

There is your monster who thinks of it as a place to which a man does not walk but into which he slinks to drink; and there is your monster who thinks of it as a place to be reached in a railway train and there to put on fine clothes for dinner and to be waited upon by Germans. There is your more amiable monster, who says: "I hear there is a good inn at Little Studley or Bampton Major. Let us go there." He waits until he has begun to be hungry, and he shoots there in an enormous automobile. There is your still more amiable monster, who in a hippo-mobile hippogriffically tools into a town and throws the ribbons to the person in gaiters with a straw in his mouth, and feels (oh, men, my brothers) that he is doing something like someone in a book. All these men, whether they frankly hate or whether they pretend to love, are the enemies of inns, and the enemies of inns are accursed before their Creator and their kind.

There are some things which are a consolation for Eden and which clearly prove to the heavily burdened race of Adam that it has retained a memory of diviner things. We have all of us done evil. We have permitted the modern cities to grow up, and we have told such lies that now we are accursed with newspapers. And we have so loved wealth that we are all in debt, and that the poor are a burden to us and the rich are an offence. But we ought to keep up our hearts and not to despair, because we can still all of us pray when there is an absolute necessity to do so, and we have wormed out the way of building up that splendid thing which all over Christendom men know under many names and which is called in England an INN.

I have sometimes wondered when I sat in one of these places, remaking my soul, whether the inn would perish out of Europe. I am convinced the terror was but the terror which we always feel for whatever is exceedingly beloved.

There is an inn in the town of Piacenza into which I once walked while I was still full of immortality, and there I found such good companions and so much marble, rooms so large and empty and so old, and cooking so excellent, that I made certain it would survive even that immortality which, I say, was all around. But no! I came there eight years later, having by that time heard the noise of the Subterranean River and being well conscious of mortality. I came to it as to a friend, and the beastly thing had changed! In place of the grand stone doors there was a sort of twirlygig like the things that let you into the Zoo, where you pay a shilling, and inside there were decorations made up of meaningless curves like those with which the demons have punished the city of Berlin; the salt at the table was artificial and

largely made of chalk, and the faces of the host and hostess were
no longer kind.

I very well remember another inn which was native to the
Chiltern Hills. This place had bow-windows, which were divided
into medium-sized panes, each of the panes a little rounded; and
these window-panes were made of that sort of glass which I will
adore until I die, and which has the property of distorting
exterior objects: of such glass the windows of schoolrooms and
of nurseries used to be made. I came to that place after many
years by accident, and I found that Orcus, which has devoured
all lovely things, had devoured this too. The inn was called "an
hotel," its front was rebuilt, the windows had only two panes
each quite enormous and flat, one above and one below, and the
glass was that sort of thick, transparent glass through which it
is no use to look, for you might as well be looking through air.
All the faces were strange except that of one old servant in the
stableyard. I asked him if he regretted the old front, and he said
"Lord, no!" Then he told me in great detail how kind the
brewers had been to his master and how willingly they had
rebuilt the whole place. These things reconcile one to the
grave.

Well, then, if walking, which has led me into this digression,
prepares one for the inns where they are worthy, it has another
character as great and as symbolic and as worthy of man. For
remember that of the many ways of walking there is one which
is the greatest of all, and that is to walk away.

Put your hand before your eyes and remember, you that have
walked, the places from which you have walked away, and the
wilderness into which you manfully turned the steps of your
abandonment.

There is a place above the Roman Wall beyond the River
Tyne where one can do this thing. Behind one lies the hospitality
and the human noise which have inhabited the town of the river
valley for certainly two thousand years. Before one is the dead
line of the road, and that complete emptiness of the moors as

they rise up towards Cheviot on the one hand and Carter Fell upon the other. The earth is here altogether deserted and alone: you go out into it because it is your business to go: you are walking away. As for your memories, they are of no good to you except to lend you that dignity which can always support a memoried man; you are bound to forget, and it is your business to leave all that you have known altogether behind you, and no man has eyes at the back of his head—go forward! Upon my soul, I think that the greatest way of walking, now I consider the matter, or now that I have stumbled upon it, is walking away.

IX

In Memory of Cecil Chesterton
(1879–1918)

[He founded and edited *The New Witness* and was, according to the late Sir Desmond MacCarthy, the best pugnacious journalist since Cobbett.]

CECIL CHESTERTON is dead. He has left the only place which we know and understand, and gone to better and more permanent things which we shall understand in our turn. Later, when the deadening effect of such a blow has passed, it will be possible to write, though hardly worthily, the panegyric which is his due. It may be possible (though I have never found such a thing possible even after the passage of many years) to express the intolerable sense of loss and grief which follows upon such a departure in us who remain. To-day I am incapable of either of these high things, but there is one thing I can do—which is to put upon record the greatness of what has gone away from us at this critical time, and the consequent loss to England which he loved and served as very few modern Englishmen in public life love and serve her.

There is a worn phrase, used indifferently of the few great and the many little when they die—that the loss is to us "irreparable." In this one case of Cecil Chesterton it is, in relation to his country, for once a word strictly true. Nothing can replace him, nor exercise the function which he exercised, nor do what he did for his country; the gravity of that judgment weighs upon me as I write so that I feel it like any other great public calamity—the loss of a battle, or a plague.

For this country is in high peril. For all the vigour of its blood, for all the heroism and the tenacity which it has displayed and will continue to display, it is yet in peril, because the peril concerns not the blood or the stock or the race, but its institutions; and by institutions, their vigour and their authority this ancient State, aristocratic in origin, lives. If they fall below a certain level of contempt and disease, with them the State falls, for all its other virtues may perish. There was no modern State the institutions of which were as strong but a generation ago as were those of this country. There is none in which so prodigious a revolution has been working. Everywhere else the tidal-wave of the late eighteenth century had swept over society and things had begun anew: but here continuity and all the strength which accompanies it, an oaken stuff, distinguished the public affairs of the English. In no other country had authority a stronger moral basis, nowhere were the servants of the State put higher in public esteem and more respected by those whom they lightly governed. All that is gone, and it is gone through the cowardice and the falsehood of those who should have been the conservators of England. When it was perceived that wealth could purchase anything from a useless honour to a vital policy, that membership of the various public bodies—particularly of the House of Commons—rendered a man immune, no matter what his treachery, meanness, swindling, or theft, there naturally arose an attraction between public affairs and whatever was worst in the State. It was inevitable that it should be so, for laws written or unwritten live by their sanctions, not by their mere statement. With amazing rapidity the thing developed until we came to the point where we are to-day. One of a victorious league of great nations, one which has presented the most marvellous picture of strained endeavour, is nominally represented by men and by a system containing those men, which men and which system have fallen beneath the level of scorn.

Now, when a State comes to this very grave pass—and history is there to show what such a pass means in the story of nations—there is one function of supreme value to the commonwealth. It is the function exercised by the man who will bring out corruption into the air: oxydize it; burn it up. But the exercise of such a function in such times can be undertaken only by, at the best, a very small number of men, at the worst by only one man or perhaps by none. For this function requires a combination of three things, each rare, and in combination, of course, much rarer still. These three things are knowledge, the power of lucidity in expression, and, lastly, courage.

Knowledge of what political corruption had become, of its incredible extent and degree, was, when Cecil Chesterton began his effort, confined almost entirely to those who benefited by that corruption. It was not in those days (I speak of about a dozen years ago, when, if I remember rightly, he wrote his first book upon the growing falsehood of public life) anything like what it is to-day. Men at the head of the State were still men reputable in private life. Their connection with finance was at least not a connection of the taking and giving of petty bribes, and there was still some moderate distinction between the political ideals of nominal opponents. Still, the thing had begun and had already reached a height sufficient for attack: and Cecil Chesterton attacked. Through him much more than through any other man, the knowledge of the rapidly increasing evil was spread, until now you may say that some thousands among our millions are well acquainted with the way in which they are governed and the sort of men that govern them. Those thousands will be turned into millions by the effect of this war and of the ludicrous election to which we are at this moment invited by the politicians and their financial masters. When the thing is thoroughly done, when the exposure is complete and the knowledge is universal, we shall be able to say that the great fruits of that time by which we hope to correct its great dangers will have been due in the main to the man who conducted this paper and who has now died as a soldier in France—after, thank God, he had lived to see the destruction of Prussia.

So much for knowledge. It is rare; but the power of lucid expression is much rarer. It is of the talents, as distinguished from virtues, the rarest of all. For twenty men who can write good rhetoric or even good verse, there is not one who can with intelligence seize at once the heart of a subject and present it in the shortest space so vividly and so framed that all his audience receives his own knowledge and are in communion with it. Look up and down the history of English Letters and see how rare is that gift. Swift had it, and Cobbett. Perhaps if you search you might find a half-dozen other names. There was certainly no one in our time who had it except my friend. I speak here of something which I know, for I myself, with I know not what labour, have attempted and have failed in the same task, and I have seen around me other men far more gifted than I, admirable at illustration and rhythm, at strong picturing of things, who have failed in this complete task of rapidity of synthesis informed by lucidity.

How formidable is the combination of this extremely rare type of genius with a sufficient knowledge!

Yet that combination would be sterile, were it not for the third quality which is the rarest of all.

Much might be written upon the strange paradox that at a moment and in a society where courage in almost every other form is conspicuous and splendid, public courage—the courage of the forum—dies away. It is inevitable. Were it not so, the peril and the decline would never have come about. So it is. Of all men who speak upon the intolerable condition of our public life, of all the hundreds and thousands of men who speak of it in tones varying from contempt to anger, only some tiny fraction dares to *print*; that is, under modern conditions, to speak publicly in the market place. And of these Cecil Chesterton was by far the highest example. His courage was heroic, native, positive, and equal: always at the highest potentiality of courage. He never in his life checked an action or a word from a consideration of personal caution, and that is more than can be said of any other man of his time. We can say of him, what is sometimes said indifferently in connection with other persons, that he was incapable of such caution; that is, the idea of it would not even occur to him. He was incapable of neglecting an act from lack of courage or even from a modification of courage, as most men are incapable of a public act which would involve them in danger, and by the measure of the one you may take the measure of the other. Courage possessed and displayed in that degree is by definition heroic.

There was no risk he would not run, no suffering which he would not encounter: from ridicule to misconception, and from misconception to imprisonment, and from imprisonment to poverty. This, the third thing necessary, gave to his talent and to his knowledge their enormous value.

All *that* his country has lost, and his country will not find such a combination again. Among public things it is a great thing, and we have lost a very great man.

There are private things which are the more important in the decline of a State. The qualities I have described move me less than the things which I have not said of such a friend and of such a companion in arms: *tam cari capitis*.

From *The New Witness*, December 13th, 1918.

On Boycotts

BOYCOTTS differ more than any other kind of social, human action in the degree of consciousness informing them. And it is because there are such a very large number of half-conscious or quarter-conscious, or even almost unconscious, boycotts in any society that most people are surprised when they hear that the boycott exists; nearly everyone, when he has a particular boycott explained to him, either indignantly denies it or tries to think of it as something other than what it is.

That is because there is something mean and unfair attaching to the idea of a boycott. It connotes hypocrisy; and people do not like to feel mean, unfair, and hypocritical. But when you come to think of it there is something to be said, if not for the morals of the boycott, at any rate for its inevitability, seeing that the boycott is impelled by two powerful social forces—the taboo, and that instinct of self-preservation which every organism, including the social organism, must exercise. The boycott is a weapon like any other. Being a weapon very suitable for particular occasions, it naturally occurs for use on those occasions, and the more a society is guilty of the habit of self-deception, the more in that society will the boycott flourish. This does not mean to say that the boycott has not also flourished immensely against certain dangers or unpopular things even in very frank straightforward societies. No society was more straightforward than that glorious military society of pagan Rome, from which we are all descended and on which we are all founded. But it exercised at least one very severe boycott, and that was the boycott against the Church. So far as the testimony of the outer world is concerned, you can hardly trace the history of the Church at all before the fourth century. What we know of it is almost entirely from within; so rigid was the instinctive boycott to which it was subjected. That society felt instinctively that it was in great peril of change, and it also instinctively felt that the right weapon against the thing menacing it was silence. Seeing that the great force of the other side was persuasion, or, as its enemies would have called it, the contagion of the mind, the obvious remedy was to put a cordon of silence round it.

There may be other contributory causes to the strange lack of external evidence upon this capital historical phenomenon of nearly three centuries between A.D. 29 and the Edict of Milan. For instance, it is clear that the dark ages would tend to preserve Christian apologetics more than they would the writings of opponents. Still, I doubt whether anything really accounts for the thing in the main except this theory of a boycott, and therein I am supported by an authority which is to-day perhaps the most learned in the matter of the Roman language, and very learned in the matter of Roman society also.

Where the taboo comes in it somewhat spoils the distinct definition of a boycott, at least as far as the inner character of the thing is concerned, though it has exactly the same external effect. When I was young there was a very strong taboo in the matter of English titles. There were special occasions when they could not be mentioned under pain of social death, and this taboo, like all sacramentals, was dressed up in a fine complexity. It was one of the main points in good breeding, to know not only when titles were taboo but when they were, on the contrary, the opposite of taboo, i.e. necessarily to be expressed. Many a young man in those days would have burnt with shame at putting the wrong form of title on an envelope, and with equal shame at mentioning the right form of title aloud in the hearing of its bearer; and the bearer would have been shocked beyond words. There are large relics of this strong taboo still remaining in the midst of our ruin of Victorian things. The Temple is unroofed, but the pillars still stand, and to this day you may see a lord go into a shop and mumble his name, instead of saying in a bold manner—

"*LORD HUMP*, and mind you put *THE EARL HUMP* on the package; don't call me a Baron!"

But I do not want to digress on taboos; I come back to the boycott. I say that when the taboo enters into the boycott it may spoil the distinct definition of the thing, but it has the same external effect, and I think that in most boycotts there is introduced, instinctively, by the combined effect of the sacramental instinct in man and of time, the element of taboo. For instance, we still boycott a description of income. You hardly ever hear a man who possesses an income above the artisan wage telling others what that income is; you hardly ever hear a man ask. This is a boycott with a very obvious reason. A man's credit, his power of getting things done, his chance of escaping burdens and a hundred other things which go to make up the comfort or discomfort of his life, depend upon his income. To exaggerate his income in some cases is an advantage to him; to pretend it is smaller than it is is, in other cases, an advantage to him; and as he does not want conflicting testimonies from his own lips and the reputation of a liar, he steers a middle course and holds his tongue. But the thing has been going on so long (at least a century, and in its present rigid form for more than a lifetime) that the sacramental idea has crept in, and the boycott of income-talk and of the income-subject is clothed with a religious feeling. The *Favete Linguis* has appeared.

One of the best proofs of this is the action of a madman in the matter. All mad people like to break one or more of the conventions (which, let me tell those who despise formal logic, is not equivalent to saying that all those who break one or more conventions are mad). What I mean is that there is an insane pleasure in shocking people, and one can surely tell by one's common sense when that pleasure is insane and when it is of a sane and merely inpertinent sort. Well, so much has the taboo got into the income-boycott that a certain class of people love to break it.

I knew a don of Oxford in my youth whose nervous disease

took this particular form: he invariably opened conversation with the lady next whom he might happen to be sitting at dinner with this phrase pronounced in a low voice: "*What is your precise income?*" It was calculated to startle, and it did. Having delivered that shell the worthy man would put on a very interested expression, not unlike that which we should see, I think, on the face of a spider when he is watching for flies; for he well knew that his victim was cut off, with only three avenues of escape open to her. If, as was usually the case, she answered by the feminine habit of ignoring the question he would chuckle gently and say: "Ha! ha! I see you don't like to admit it!" If she got angry and said it was none of his business, his pleasure was so indecently obvious that he scored. If (as was the case with some witty women, who had strayed into the university from outside) she answered with an exact figure (a wrong one of course), he would arch his eyebrows in surprise and say: "Oh, surely more than *that*!" Such was the simple pleasure of his old age. After all, every man must have his hobby.

Among boycotts duly to be classified in its right place and pigeon-holed is the personal boycott; and this is a most fascinating subject. I do not mean the boycott of a man in the sense of keeping him out of people's houses: I mean the boycott of his name, a sort of conspiracy to do the opposite of booming him: an understanding that he is not to be advertised. But one has to be very careful indeed in the testing and appreciation of this specimen, because there is nothing on which judgment goes more wrong. There is always a tendency to think that those of whom we are fond are being unduly boycotted; and since men are a great deal fonder of themselves than of anyone else (not so women), they tend, if they do not get all the booming they want, to think they are being boycotted. But though nine times out of ten the thing is a delusion, the tenth time it has an element of truth. And it would be a most interesting piece of analysis to discover the complex of motives which establishes these boycotts. For instance, there was the distinct boycott of Samuel Butler:

I mean Samuel Butler the lesser, the modern one. It is no good saying it was merely the oddness of the man, his retirement, and all the rest of it. It was much more than that. It was an instinctive action on the part of many and a conscious action on the part of a few, undertaken to save a religion. The materialism of Butler's day was a religion. Its expression in philosophy (which is called "Science") was also a religion. Now you may notice that religions never mind a stupid opponent; they whet their teeth upon him; or, to use a better metaphor, they live upon him: they eat him and digest him. But an opponent who has really found a weak point is quite another matter, and Butler had found a weak point in the Religion of Materialism. The real value of his attack may be summed up in that famous judgment of his that, "A hen was a roundabout way to get one egg to lay another egg." Therein you have the whole philosophy of creation—in that famous ironic judgment of his. And the whole of the intellectual drawing-rooms *en masse* closed up like a flock of sheep to resist invasion. They did not in the least mind the English curates and bishops who wanted to believe (for some reason best known to them-selves) that all the animals were separately made out of bits of mud, as it were with fingers; but the philosophical attack (unanswerable in my eyes) they dreaded—and hence, I do believe, the boycott of Samuel Butler. There was also, for other reasons and on other fashions, a partial boycott of Burton. Here again I mean Burton the lesser, the modern, not the *Anatomy of Melancholy* man.

Boycotts can be broken down, and it would be a further point of interest to survey what boycotts have succeeded in stifling their object and what have failed. The one against the Church failed lamentably, as we all know, and when the pressure was taken off by Constantine, the bound upwards was all the more remarkable. And the boycott of a person can also be broken, especially by industry on the part either of himself or of his friends. But I fancy that, on the average, the boycott is more successful than unsuccessful, and this conclusion fills me with gloom. Which reminds me (by way of conclusion) that it would really be a pleasant thing, for a change, to come to any conclusion that did not fill one with gloom! I look at the young people going about the streets, and I wonder whether they are as cheerful as I was at their age . . . or is it all put on?

XI

Children's Books

FOR a very long time—how many hundred years nobody knows—children had for their literature work of a certain type. They still have work of that type for their literature, and perhaps fifty or sixty years hence, when such a thing as a market for children's books shall be forgotten, they will continue to have literature of the same type, and so on, until the heavens open and things come to an end. That type we all know. It is of two branches, verse and prose. The characteristics of the verse are terseness, simplicity, improbability and finality as to theme, strongly emphasized lilt—something indelible for the memory as to form. For instance:

> *Here lies Elizabeth Holloway Dent:*
> *She kicked up her heels and away she went.*
> *Whither she went or how she fares,*
> *Nobody knows and nobody cares.*

It should further be remarked that the theme is not so important as the manner. Some of these rhymes are actually meaningless, such as the "counting out" rhymes. None of them suffer any complexity of incident, nor end upon a third (still less a seventh), but always upon the keynote.

The second half of this kind of literature is the story in prose, and the characteristics of this are equally clear. There must always be injustice and peril, the one overcome, the other solved in the end. This is even true of the jocular stories where some sense of justice satisfied is always apparent. It is further true that no incident, person, or thing is introduced into these stories unless that incident or person or thing serves the purpose of the plot. Thus it is a canon in all this sort of literature that there are no descriptions of scenery or discussions upon society and morals.

Now, in the very ephemeral phase of society through which we are unhappily passing, and which demands regular books for children, those permanent things in prose and verse which childhood has demanded and will demand can guide us. I will suppose that you are a poor man or woman (you will not bear me a grudge? It is but an hypothesis. Nay, nay! not a word), and that of two forms of dishonour you prefer forcing a child's story out of yourself to tapping some other impecunious friend, and that you have not the heroism to die or to go to the workhouse. If this is your circumstance, the advice you should take is clear. In order to write for children in verse or in prose, do what your long ancestry did and what your long posterity will do: give them those rhymes and give them those stories. And if you can't, don't.

But you can. There is no one that cannot tell some sort of story to a child and very few that cannot make up some sort of rhyme for a child, if only they will remember that the rhyme must have those qualities and the prose those other qualities which we have just seen. As to writing really good rhymes and really good stories, that is, of course, no more to be taught, and such a gift is no more to be analysed, than the corresponding gift of thumbnail sketching. A very few people can do it. All the remaining millions cannot do it; and those who can do it have no idea what it is in them that gives them such a power.

Nevertheless, even for those who can do it, there is one plain rule, although it is a negative one: which is, never to embroider, and never to be "on one side" whether through irony or by any other form of allusion. You can, of course, if you like have a parallel in your mind, and you can be trying to teach another lesson than that which your story may convey to the child. That is your own business. But, if you allow any such things to come in between you and your childish audience, you are done for. Children know exactly where they are in matters of the soul, and so would each of us if we had not lost our innocence somewhere about the time of the first Home Rule Bill, or the great

Dock Strike at the latest. The presentation of matters which a child cannot comprehend is just as bad art in this department as is that detestable habit in criticism of sticking in bits of foreign languages which your reader knows nothing of: with the added drawback, that your reader if he is grown up will not openly complain; but the child will.

Now someone may say to me: "If this is so, what about the success of *Gulliver's Travels*, Hans Andersen, and *The Rose and the Ring*?" The answer is simple enough. Andersen's stories and Thackeray's tale are stories which a child can read as stories by themselves; and the fact that the author, being a grown man, has chosen to wink at other grown-ups in the telling does not interfere at all with the straightforward tale, which alone the child demands. In *The Rose and the Ring* you have peril overcome and injustice righted. That Thackeray had in his mind a few rather silly hobbies of his own, no one who knows the man or the period can doubt. He is praising his own class, having a dig at the monastic institution, showing his newspaper dislike of the Russians, his natural ignorance of what a real monarchy could be, and twenty other mental habits of his class and his generation. But he is so excellent a workman, or, to be more accurate, so vivid an artist, that he cannot help writing a good clear story all the same.

Gulliver's Travels is a still better example of what I mean. No child cares twopence about Laputa, and I never met one who cared about the Houyhnhnms. But when it comes to all the adventures among very little people and very big people, there you have exactly what the child wants; and note that there is peril overcome in both those stories, and, to some extent, injustice put right. But the child does find dreary passages even here, and skips them (as, for instance, the King of the Giants moralizing over the wickedness and insignificance of men).

Which leads me to two last considerations, the element of wonder in children's stories and the element of morals. As to the element of morals, we have already had the prime element of injustice to be put right. That you must always have, because the sense of justice is the basis of any moral teaching, and it is especially the clearest thing in a child's creed. It is, for instance, the weakness of Lewis Carroll's books that the man did not love justice and that you have no iniquity redressed, but unfortunately a little spitefulness now and then against the sense of justice. For the world in which he lived was at once a privileged and a timid world. But one may fearlessly adventure into plain moral teaching of all kinds and please an audience of children immensely thereby, so long as the thing is done through the vehicle of a story. For instance, one may show the misadventures of a coward or of a boastful man to the great delight of children, and in connection with this it is always well to put in a good dose of violence.

As to wonder, that is a more subtle business. The child can get his wonder out of almost anything so long as the picture he is asked to construct is outside the immediate connotation of his materials. You see this with toys. Give a child a few bricks and tell him to make a steam-engine out of them, and he is perfectly content. He can imagine his steam-engine doing all that a steam-engine can do, and more. Give him a little model engine and, if there can be no doubt of its being quite out of nature, either by its tiny size or by its makeshiftedness, he will get much the same enjoyment. But rich people who have fallen into such errors will bear me out when I say that to give a child a very large and perfect model of a locomotive, is inimical to this power of make-believe in which the child satisfies his appetite for wonder.

Now, so is it with your story for children. Bring in conventional machinery—a King, a Dragon, a Princess—and the child will eagerly seize such food and convert it into the flesh and blood of Romance. Elaborate your description, and you do but spend words upon an attempt, such as must be made for more jaded imaginations, to call up a whole costume at the expense of many words, and the child will reject what you offer him.

Beyond this there is, of course, the magic of emotions which we have retained ourselves from childhood, and which we should, if we have good memories, be able to express in simple phrases. There are few phrases more impressive of distance, adventure, and revelation than the old lilting phrase "over the hills and far away." And there are perhaps a dozen such phrases in the language, more prosaic, which have similar connotations. Such is the classic gambit: "Once upon a time"; or, again, a phrase I have always remembered from a book of my own childhood: "And they sailed and they sailed till they came to an island."

All the world knows that incantation and the repetition of rhythmical phrases—especially in triple repetition—contribute to a sense of wonder. Time in fashioning the older fairy stories has attended to that rule.

There is one last canon which is, that if, in writing a story or verses for a child, you have not in your own mind a bright picture of the thing you are telling, then you are certainly on the way to failure, and had better leave off; for, while it is true of all fiction and of all verse, it is particularly true of verse and fiction of this kind that, though there is no positive rule for the communication of one mind to another, yet this negative rule is universally true: where the mind has not conceived it cannot bring forth, and unless you see and hear before you write or as you write, your writing is vain.

XII

Silchester in 1912

IT is one year ago, almost, as I write, since I first saw Silchester. I went there to recover the Port-Way, which is a Roman road running from Silchester to Old Sarum. I had read in the writings of a don at Oxford that it had disappeared for ever in the neighbourhood of Silchester. This was almost enough to convince me that it would stick out of the ground conspicuously like a railway embankment. When I got there I did not find it sticking out so clearly as all that, but I found it clearly enough marked at short intervals from Silchester onwards. All this is by the way; for I am not writing of this Roman road (which I will plot out as dully as I can in the atlas of such things which I am making), but of Silchester itself.

I desire to convey to those who read this, something of what filled my own mind when I first saw the place just before the Christmas holidays of last year. I am not at all hopeful that I shall succeed in that transference of emotion from mind to mind. For there is here a bridge to be built over a very wide chasm. In one state of mind Silchester would seem to be nothing but a very large field with a bit of very old wall around it; in another state of mind it is all Europe.

The scheme of Europe changes exceedingly slowly. It changes so slowly that I would rather think of it as a sort of swinging, majestically moving forth and back again. Very few of its ancient cities wholly fail. Very few new ones permanently arise. You can go back, back, back in history, and see Europe always itself, finding, as at Arles, town under town almost as deep as you can dig a well—or as at Ilion. But here and there, as though to enhance this permanence, you get desolation. You have it in Silchester. And precisely because that desolation is absolute do you feel more strongly the greatness of the past from which we came and which made us.

For Silchester is but a great field lying open to the sky, with not one fragment left above the stubble or the plough or the fallow of winter; and round it all about still runs the ruined wall, and outside the wall the ditch, though silted in for centuries, is deep and sharp still.

I may put it this way: Any man coming to Silchester from without would see that he was coming up at the ruin of something. Yet once past the low boundary of that ruin, past the remaining lower courses of the stone wall, and you are in a blank emptiness. Everything has gone.

Outside the wall to the north the Amphitheatre stood, the place where the games were the necessary symbol of fellowship in every Roman city. It had an arena fifty yards across. It was a great thing, for Silchester was in its way a great city. How many families it guarded we cannot tell, but converging on this place came at least four of the great roads, perhaps five, and the Feast Days must have been crowded things. This old theatre is now wholly hidden by earth and on one side entirely broken down. It looks (as you come upon it) like nothing but a big mound such as are the mounds upon which some of our castles were built—at Oxford, for instance. It is covered with trees, and it is only when you have climbed the ridge so wooded, which wholly covers the ruined stones, and have looked down upon the arena within, that the model of the thing strikes you. It gives one (after Nîmes, Orange, the Paris ruins) an amazing effect of silence, seeing how full it once was, and for how long, of cheering thousands, and how now it is in perfectly abandoned fields.

From here (as, indeed, from every part of the wall and its neighbourhood) you look over a great view. Not that Silchester stands very high, but it was cunningly chosen by the tribe, which first made that place its stronghold, for survey. There is here something which you will see repeated in other similar centres —Bavai, for instance; Bavai the hub of a whole wheel of roads.

Bavai is not deserted to-day; it is only very much decayed. Yet it suggests the site of Silchester; standing on the flat top of a roll of land that is rather low than high, that is approached by a very slight long slope every way, and that none the less commands the countryside every way for miles and miles.

How well one can understand the manner in which the place must have been a goal and an object when all those roads were used and when Silchester was the capital of its district. How men must have come up those miles of plumb straight highways and have seen, half a day before they reached it, the roofs (perhaps, at the end of the Empire, the domes) of Calleva. There was a magnificence about the place which its size and sundry things discovered teach us still in spite of that fashion for denying the Roman basis of England; a fashion which, like so much that has sprung from religious fanaticism, warps English history still.

For Silchester when it was alive was not only larger than, or as large as, the Paris of Julian, but it had splendour in its public buildings. Its great courthouse was not much shorter than Westminster Hall as we see it to-day. If we are to judge by the fragments of the pillars and by the lighting which it must have had, it may have been higher than Westminster Hall—it must, at the least, have been nearly as high—and if we are wise we will believe that the Roman town was altogether upon this scale.

It is half a mile as you look from the North Wall southwards to the southern gate. It is half a mile as you look eastwards from the Western Wall towards the church and the farmhouse which are the solitary roofs beyond the emptiness on the farther side. You had there, then, something like a third of Roman London; or perhaps more like a quarter, for the outline is not square but irregular. All this great place has utterly disappeared.

I have said that a complete desolation of this sort is very rare in Britain. I think there is only one other example of it, which is Wroxeter, under the Wrekin. The towns maintained their continuous life; Lincoln and London and Winchester and Canterbury and York and Manchester and Carlisle and Gloucester and

Worcester and Colchester, and I know not how many others. But Silchester has gone altogether. How did it go? No one can tell you that. So far as one can make out, it decayed and was at last deserted; largely, I should fancy, through the breakdown of the roads. But, at any rate, it did decay and it was deserted. And when the Middle Ages arose after the enormous gap, with their fairly full records, Calleva of the Atrebates had gone for ever.

Still the question recurs to me, and never have I been able so much as to begin to solve it. How did those towns disappear; the two that went in England, the many that disappeared abroad? What happened to Ruscino under the Canigou—big enough to give its name to a whole province? How did Bibracte die? How Alesia? You must not think that they were barbarous strongholds naturally given up when the Romans taught men to build better and in better places. In each of them you may see by its remains that the place was one of the places of the Empire—yet each has altogether gone!

How utterly Hippo has disappeared I have written in another place. Almost as utterly has Cæsarea of Barbary.

Some say that the stone is carted away for local use. Like enough! But what of the foundations? And how is it that you so often find, in these lost towns of the Empire, nothing but little weak foundations which were obviously no more than the supports of huts and ramshackle houses in the last stages of the decline. It is a common thing to discover, wherever a Roman town has disappeared, that the traces left are those of a few very flimsy walls and large gardens about every house; that is, when even so much evidence remains. What came before that last stage? Why was the magnificence of the place abandoned and, most puzzling of all, where did the materials go? They seem in Silchester to have preserved something of their great Town Hall till quite, quite late. Perhaps they had a religious feeling about it; perhaps the fragments were too big or too splendid for the use of marauders. Some of the slabs of the marble that encrusted it have lain there all these thousands of years—part of it from

Purbeck, part from the Pyrenees. They have found some drums of the pillars too—but where is all the rest?

Where, for that matter, is the town that there was about Lugdunum high on the Garonne; or who could steal, or for what purpose, the massive barracks of Lambese? Yet they have gone. Many lessons of mortality have been drawn by men, many emblems, many mysteries of it noted. None as a lesson or an emblem or a mystery is like these few lost towns. Of them, in England, Silchester is the chief marvel, a marvel to any man's hand, in reach of every man.

XIII

A Couplet

WHEN a man sails down the northern coast of Sicily, going east to west from the Straits of Messina towards Trapani, he passes by a series of strong headlands, high and dark, which rise straight from the sea and open one after the other in successive capes upon his journey. When he has so proceeded for the greater part of his voyage, about half a day's sail before the main harbour of Palermo, he will note a most striking rocky hill, very high, detached from the main run of the highlands, and jutting out towards the shore, under the farther edge of which lies a sort of shelter rather than a haven: a shelter against the Levanter and all the strong winds between north and west round by east. This towering great rock, this haven, are the rock and the haven of Cefalu, which take their name by corruption from the original Greek word meaning a "head"; for this mighty mass of stone has just this outline as you come upon it from the east before rounding into its nook of shelter.

Here one of the early Norman kings, caught in a storm, vowed while he was yet in peril to build a church if he could make land, and finding refuge under the lee of the great height duly performed his vow.

He set up the church, which still stands; and in it, round the half dome of the apse above the high altar, he had affixed a most majestic mosaic of Our Lord in Glory coming to Judgment, and underneath that awful portraiture he caused to be fixed, also in mosaic, two Latin lines, the one a hexameter, the other a pentameter. All this was done in the lifetime before the year 1200: that is, some seven and a half centuries ago. And there they stand to this day, quite unchanged, for mosaic is the most enduring of all ornament.

It is upon these lines that I would write here. They are as follows:

FACTUS HOMO, FACTOR HOMINIS, FACTIQUE REDEMPTOR
    JUDICO CORPOREUS CORPORA CORDA DEUS

This couplet seems to me to sum up more completely than any other statement of similar length the whole Catholic Doctrine of the Incarnation, its intention and consequence.

Now, who wrote it?

Let me translate it here, very imperfectly and at far too great a length—but expansion is necessary to translate the intimate meanings:

"I, who was made man and who was the maker of man, and who am the Redeemer of what I made

"Being of human frame, do judge the bodies and the hearts of men: and I am God."

I say it is impossible in any translation to give the original, and in a thing as powerful as this the impossibility is manifest. Terseness, packing your meaning, is the very essence of power in metrical statement, and I suppose this quality of terseness could nowhere be found more triumphant than in these stupendous lines. Were I to expand the translation further, I might the more bring out the depths of the original. Thus the two words "corpora corda" imply the bodily appetites, the physical actions, the outward energies of men, and also their thoughts and their affections, their loyalties and treasons, their faith and their despair. While the word "Deus" at the end means not only God, nor only "And I am God," but still more, "For I am also God"; and on the top of this the word "Deus" is final in meaning as in position. It sums up the whole affair, and clinches down the proclamation, giving it complete substance and full stature. The verses are an amazing thing altogether.

Who wrote that couplet? Or if we do not know the name of the man who wrote it, where is it first to be found?

I have spent a great deal of trouble in the way of research over a great many things in the course of my life. I have worked for long hours to discover the epitaph of Caedwalla, King of Sussex and of the Isle of Wight and of Hampshire, which stood in Old St. Peter's, and is supposed to be still in the crypt of New St. Peter's to-day in Rome. I have tried to trisect the plane angle, and I have discovered, to my immense joy and to the confusion of wicked men, the direct allusion to Ebion in Origen. But I have never been able to find the source of these two Latin lines.

No doubt it is lying open to my hand, and my ignorance will seem absurd to those who know better; but I have done my best, and I have failed. I asked the late Professor Phillimore, who knew more about Christian Latin verse than any other man, what he could discover about it, and he confessed himself baffled. It might conceivably be St. Bernard, but that authorship would be rather early, for it would be almost contemporary. It is more likely to be a thing of deeper antiquity. Or is it conceivably the flash of some genius, who wrote these two lines only, and of whom nothing else is known?

The great painter John Sargent, wandering in these parts, read those lines many years ago, and he put them (with one small change, which I regret) under that inspired Crucifixion of his in the public library at Boston: so true is it that reality strikes a chord throughout the world. Save in the public library at Boston and this church in Cefalu, I know no other place where they may be publicly read and pondered. It is a pity, for they ought to be everywhere.

The lines will remain as powerful as ever, whether their author is known or unknown. Indeed, they may be much better known than I imagine. But they have haunted me for years as something singular, and will so haunt me, I suppose, till I die, and afterwards.

XIV

The Immortal Artist

I READ the other day an article of the greatest interest by Mr. Nevinson upon himself and his colleagues in his craft, in which article he said two things of outstanding effect. The first was a quotation from some judgment or other, that art was produced by man in an unconscious effort or appetite to cheat mortality. The other was that our modern artists, though too much pre-occupied with death, no longer wish to be immortal.

As to the first of these pronouncements (it was not the writer's own, but attributed to another), I cannot agree. The essential motive of art, as it seems to me, is the rendering permanent of beauty in spite of change and time. A man does not primarily try to paint well, or to write good verse, or to build beautifully, because he does not think himself personally immortal, and is therefore secretly urged to put up a sort of simulacrum of himself, a sort of image, his works, to last when he shall have wholly ceased to be. Great work has been done by those who accepted and those who denied the personal immortality of man. And, on the whole, more has been done by those who accept it than those who deny. Indeed, I think it may be said historically that, just as the great mass of the human race have lived under the conception of immortality, so have the great mass of good artists. When a man desires, as normal and healthy men should, that good work, and therefore their own good work, should be very lasting, it is not as a foil to despair or to indifference. It is rather a recognition of something in man which is not subject to time; a boast that man can render permanent one moment of that flux which is the condition of all things about him and even of his own self in body and mood, if not of the mysterious inward core.

There is here a cousinship between plastic art and history. The determination to establish record is the same in both; and you may note this curious separate point of sameness in both, that each is vitally concerned with reality, because each instinctively appreciates that reality is a condition of permanence. However much draughtsmen pretend that they are unconcerned with the likeness of their image to the object, they always fall back, even the most affected of them, in their unguarded moments upon the natural expression of copying and mimicry and substitution from which all plastic art springs. And what architect will waste himself upon perishable material? Who will build in cardboard when he can build in stone? It is the same with record. A man who desires reputation as an historian is perpetually defending his character for judgment and his right vision of reality. He must even be concerned (though it is of little moment) with the examiner's detail of accuracy in the infinitesimals. He is annoyed with so slight a thing as a misprint or a slip of the pen.

Here, also, the truth comes out in the unguarded moments of the most devitalized academic attempter at history, just as it comes out in the unguarded moments of the most affected painter. The painter, after a hundred phrases affirming that external reality is indifferent to him, and that he cares nothing for likeness, will be caught saying of another man's work, "Who ever saw a cow like that?" or "It has movement: you can see the cloud coming at you," or "It's absurdly flat." And in each of those sentences he betrays his intimate criterion, and admits that the picture of a cow ought not to recall a crocodile, that the vivid sensation of motion is a triumph when it is effected through the medium of something still, because motion is true; and that things, being solid, should be painted solid.

So with the historian. After a hundred phrases in which he pretends, after the sceptical fashion of our day, that history is all selection and that you can make of it what you please, he will say of a rival that "he never understood his Louis XI" or that "he could never get into the skin of the sixteenth century." (Actors, if you will allow me for a moment to digress on *their*

art, have the great advantage that they simply cannot, by definition, wander into all this tomfoolery of unreality. It is their
prime business to imitate. The better they do it, the greater
actors they are. I do not think that the disease can attack the stage,
for it would be so quickly mortal that it would be checked at its
first beginning by dreadful examples of financial ruin. You can
bamboozle the snobbish millionaire or corporation to buy a
hideous piece of sculpture or a nonsensical painting; but you
can't bamboozle five hundred people into sitting out three hours
of crashing boredom and paying for it the hard-earned shillings
of the middle class.)

Now, the immediate object of the artist being to fix the
reality of a moment and render it permanent (especially the
beauty of a moment), what place does the survival of his work
and name take in his general motive? I think normally a large
one. I agree with Mr. Nevinson that the modern artist does not
feel or express the desire for immortality as his seniors did. But
that is because the time in which we live is abnormal. Normally
the artist desires fame; as, indeed, do normally nearly all men.

To-day there is some disgust with fame because it has been tarn-
ished by a nauseating vulgarity. This is partly a mechanical effect
which will soon pass and is due to the novel rapidity of our
means of communication. It is much more due to the absence
of a common and positive philosophy sustaining society, to that
anarchy of standards in the whirl of which we live. That also
will pass. There has not ever been, nor, I suppose, can be, any
prolonged phase of society not morally stable. But though the
present chaos will pass, we do not know now long it will take
to pass.

The novel rapidity of communication in ideas, as in things,
has forced the control of fame into few hands and has given to
the few controlling centres a power of mechanical publicity
which, compared even with the immediate past, is gigantic. Any
name and any achievement, or lack of achievement, can be
presented in a moment to half the world, and can be hammered

in with such persistent and unchanging repetition as makes its effect fixed by torture. Let the main newspapers of a dozen capital cities follow such a "boom," and the trick is done. The kind of people who want fame of that sort are, I should almost say, "by definition," fifth-rate: incapable of doing anything worth doing, and negligible. This does not mean that the kind of people who *get* such intolerable publicity are negligible. The greatest artists often get it. But it is hardly conceivable that a man should have high creative talent without being at the same time repelled by the intolerable vulgarity of sham mechanical-ized fame. He would rather wait a hundred years. But is there anyone who does not, at the end of no matter how long an obscurity, desire his work to have glory? I doubt it. I have never met such a man. I do not think that nature could produce such a man. And I think that a man can only turn himself into such a man by that non-natural effort towards things above temporal things and intangible which is called the effort at holiness. That does, indeed, kill the desire for fame; and so, perhaps, in white-hot moments does violent temporal affection. "Que mon nom soit flétri et que la France vive!" Or, again: "Those lovers cared not whether they were immortal, for they lived in an eternal hour."

I am afraid I have quoted it before, but it will bear repetition if I refer my good, kind, and tolerant reader to a better and terser passage on immortality in artistic fame than any other I know. It is in Mr. Max Beerbohm's *Seven Men*. Read of the chap who sold his soul to the devil, and what he found in the British Museum catalogue about himself, in small print and in modern-ized spelling, as it was to appear long after his death. That will teach you something—dear, kind, tolerant reader.

XV

On Teeth

Ill fares the head, to hastening ills a prey,
Where chins accumulate and teeth decay.

TEETH enter human life in many, in varied ways. I defy any man to find a formula which shall correlate the many ways wherein Teeth apply to immortal man.

But in the lack of a formula we can at least catalogue after the fashion of the moderns, who find chaotic accumulation an easier task than thinking out a philosophy. Let me pursue the easier task.

There is the value of Teeth in theological argument. It has never been properly developed. Just at this moment, when one group of nations is slowly swinging back to orthodoxy, another is losing what little grip it had upon Theology. In this second group of nations nothing is more commonly used against the existence of a personal God than the presence of Evil. It is the champion horse these people ride whose goal is the absence of motive in the world.

Now, to both these arguments Teeth are an admirable support. If they have not been used in that argument as they should be, it is due, I am sure, to the stupidity of the sectaries in question.

There are two practical arguments against the universal goodness so far as man is concerned. The first I leave to the man with the Muck Rake, who is no longer a friend of mine, for he has really made himself impossible lately, in verse and in prose (and so have his wife and daughter); but the second is to be found in Teeth.

Man, born of woman, and having these few years in which to battle along—I was going to say "through the daylight," but it has become very dim—is burdened grotesquely with Teeth.

They have a purpose, it is true. They are useful for chewing—well and good. They are useful also (in simple and straight-forward societies) for the expression of emotion, as when the hero "unlips his Teeth"; they have some slight use for offensive purposes as a weapon—but it is very slight.

Teeth also keep the mouth stern, and lend a certain dignity to the face while they remain. When Teeth are gone there is a looseness. Also Teeth are agents of the will, as when one shall clench his Teeth (but grinding is as dead as mutton).

Added to these uses there is use in articulation. Your toothful man speaks the more clearly. But when you have numbered these uses all is said.

Now consider the drawbacks! They interfere with decent looks, for they are often discoloured or (and) misshapen. They stick forward, and in other ways disfigure their unfortunate owners. Next, and much worse, they ache. They ache to no purpose. They do not ache because you have abused them or done them wrong, nor to warn you against something you should avoid. Still less do they ache as a punishment for wrong-doing. That they leave to the heart. They ache in pure sport, anarchic-ally, wantonly. They usually ache worse in youth, while we are still innocent and when we have not yet abused the main physical laws. I think—but I am not quite sure—that on the whole they ache worse with good people than with bad people, and upon this I suggest there should be drawn up (by order of some politician living off the taxes) a statistical report, with curves and parallel columns and simple algebraical formulæ, and all that is required for your True Statistical Report. It would be far more valuable than most of their Blue Books, for toothache is a real plague, whereas most of the things they bother about are diseases which, without much pain, rid us of the burden of this detestable life.

Teeth are so much of an anomaly that they may, I repeat, be

used with power against the theology of our fathers, which will also be, poor reader (and you will be startled to hear it), the theology of our grandsons.

Next, there is this about Teeth. Geologians have them for a sheet-anchor. Your Geologian will discover a beast with a skull like a wart-hog, legs like a giraffe, a tail like a mermaid, no back-bone, and large wings ending in claws. So far so good. He will give this animal—this fossil, to be more accurate—a name compounded from a lexicon. He will call him, for instance, the Morotherium, from Moros, signifying a Geologian, and Therium, a wild beast (compare "Deer" Grimm's Law, and all the rest of it).

The Geologian will do these things not having the fear of God before his eyes, nor that of our Lord the King, his Crown and dignity. But having found that this strange monster has a "Tooth" nearly resembling the Tooth of a mouse, your Geologian will swear by all his abandoned Gods that his morotherium is a mouse and nothing but a mouse.

The poor devil had wings with claws, a wart-hog's face and a mermaid's tail. None of these are mouse-like. Nevertheless, because his Tooth is mousewise, in among the mice he goes!

How often have we not read: "The molar, however, is a true human molar," and we are therefore compelled to regard the tumpty-tumpty skull as a true human skull. Yes! Though that skull be made up of pieces that do not fit, and are about as human as my lady's pet ape, Jacko!

The Tooth, for some reason I have never understood, fascinates your Geologian. It is to him what a human voice is to less instructed men. The dying (uninstructed) man says, feebly: "I can no longer see; but I hear . . . I hear . . . the beloved voice." Thereby is he certain of the beloved presence. None other has that tone. It is the soul that speaks—so the Geologian with his Tooth. All else may dissemble, but not the Tooth. And with what pleasure do they not appal young men and women with the story of the Bird that had Teeth, proving thereby beyond a doubt that it was a Transitional Bird, a Bird in the making, a Bird not yet arrived.

Teeth have their place in oaths, but oaths are disreputable things and I will not introduce them here. Teeth, also (for some reason I have never understood), are adjunctive to lies. That a man should lie in his throat is ill thought of, but when he lies in his Teeth it is beyond bearing. Teeth also are addressed as are no other parts of the body. There was once a current expression (it has gone out lately, but would come in very useful, I think, at Westminster during their debates, if ever their debates should attain any interest again), "I say it in your *teeth*", or "to your *teeth*."

It is a powerful expression. I have a vague recollection that it was used by Henry IV in the process of his usurpation, but I may be wrong. I will leave to my reader the labour of discovering the reference.

Teeth also have a certain mechanical value in verse. All my contemporaries who write verse have to deal with two words, "Truth" and "Youth." Now I find it deplorably common that no rhyme to Youth is used by them except Truth, and (rarely) the absurd word "Ruth." They have forgotten "Tooth." It is the same way with "World." "World" is an admirable sound to put in at the end of a line, and most of our great modern poets leave themselves compelled to match it with "furled," "curled," or "hurled." But there are other words—which I shall not write down here for fear of losing the monopoly. So it is with good old "Truth" and "Youth." "Ruth" is silly. It is a snag. It pulls the reader up sharply by its absurdity. But what is the matter with Tooth?

> Whose stark ungrateful age had felt the Tooth
> Of tumpty-tumpty, tumpty-tumpty Youth

exactly describes (filling in, of course, the blanks with any adjectives convenient) the sensations of an elderly man chucked sideways by the energies of the young.

It is curious how little this use of Tooth has been appreciated. I have even known the word "booth" dragged in by the hair, though it does not rhyme at all because the "th" is sharp. Yet there was Tooth waiting for them all the time, and none of them ever used it! They may even go down to the lowest depths and use "forsooth" or "good sooth." I came across one modern once who used "newth," meaning newness, and made it rhyme with "youth." And yet there was Tooth lying humbly to his hand, had he not been blind to so honourable a servant.

And what more of Teeth? Why, an infinite amount did space allow.

There is the exaggeration of Teeth when they become tusks; which word, by the way, would make a very useful telephone call whenever they needed something parallel to, but different from, Trunks. They would have done well to call Toll "Tusks." In that connection your Tooth leads off into the whole great field of Ivory on the one hand and the long story of the wild boar on the other. It becomes the machinery for Venus and Adonis. It is the Oliphant of Roland. But talking of Roland, there was another Tooth in that business. For in the jewelled rim of Roland's Oliphant (which was a great Tooth) stood a smaller Tooth, which was, as you will remember, the Tooth of St. Peter; and it was a Tooth of a large size which the seafarer from the North showed to King Alfred in proof of his voyage, saying: "Look at that!"

Teeth also were used for a seal, better than thumb marks: "and the angry King of England pressed his front teeth upon the wax saying: 'This sign cannot be denied.'"

The subject is endless. Of False Teeth the censor forbids me to speak—and naturally enough, for it is a tender subject with him. But tell me, idiot singer, how and why have Teeth ever been compared with pearls? What on earth have they in common with pearls? Pearls are dull, grey, opaque, small, and round. Teeth are nothing of the kind.

The matter crowds upon me. I desire to talk of the breaking

of Teeth in the Psalms, and of Convocation and its veto upon that expression. I desire to talk of the Teeth that are in the Alps, the Tooth of the South and the Tooth of Ice. I desire to talk of trees that were torn by the Teeth of the Wild Man of Lebanon; of Harold, also, whose Tooth was blue. But all art consists of limitation and a knowledge of the end.

XVI

The Pilgrims' Way

THE main "ways" of human communication, most of which are still standing even upon our modern maps, came into existence through different causes: they were established by trade and according to the different methods of carriage which that trade used; they were established by armies, whose motive was also, in the long run, economic; but there were other motives as well which are to-day somewhat neglected, and the principal of these was religion. Many of the great tracks of the world were partly called into being by the desire to reach a holy place and to return from it in the easiest fashion.

A comparatively recent example of this is the road to Mecca from the north, and the present railway to Medina. There was some such track, of course, from north to south, centuries before the Mohammedan movement began; but its great importance, and the fact that it is now actually followed by a railway, is in part based upon the religious motive. It goes through places that are on the edges of the desert and mark the ends of the caravan routes; all the way from Aleppo and Damascus to Mecca that road and that subsequent railway to Medina have arisen, partly through commercial and military need, but also because men desired to come and worship in great numbers at a shrine.

We have in England an example of the same kind in the old pilgrims' road to Canterbury from the west—"The Pilgrims' Way." This also is a mixed example, because the first trace of the road upon which the later use was based was presumably not religious in foundation but commercial. Though it dates from long before the beginning of our recorded history, we may fairly affirm that this old British road leading from Salisbury Plain to Canterbury arose from the necessities of travel, and particularly of transport. Later there was developed a branch road leading into it from Winchester and joining the first road at Farnham. Thenceforward, after a stretch of sand, it ran along the southern dry escarpment of the chalk to Canterbury, whence roads branched out like the spokes of a wheel to the sheltered water of the Wensum, to the haven of Dover, and to that of the Portus Lemanis (Lympne).

This ancient way having been trodden by men and flocks, by travellers and by armies, for we know not how many centuries, became partially superseded by the newer roads which came into being with the Roman administration in the first century and with the gradual growth of the subsidiary ways connected with these. At the end of the twelfth century, however, the old way got a new use and a new name. It became in its whole length the easiest continuous track for men to follow who from the west sought the shrine of St. Thomas à Becket at Canterbury. (The reader will, I hope, excuse my preference for the traditional form of the name and my repugnance to pedantic modern changes in the use of it.) St. Thomas had been murdered at the end of December 1170. He was at once venerated as a martyr throughout Christendom, and within a few weeks the stream of pilgrimage to his shrine had set in. It flowed without ceasing until the end of the first third of the sixteenth century—three hundred and fifty years.

The natural rallying-point for such pilgrimage from the south of England was the considerable centre of Winchester, which had until comparatively lately been the capital of south England, and from Winchester onwards those who sought Canterbury were provided by the old British Trackway with an established guide, following which they could not miss the best soil—that is, the dryest—and the easiest crossings of the rivers, which avoided marsh and brushwood and undergrowth, and which took them, on the whole, by the shortest line.

This usage of the old way as a pilgrimage road permanently changed its name. There were many other pilgrimage ways, connected with other shrines, and even a few others connected with Canterbury; some of these were tributaries, as it were, leading into the old way from lesser centres; but when one speaks of "The Pilgrims' Way" in recent English history one means the ancient trail from Winchester to Canterbury, much of which is now incorporated in modern hard roads but most of which is still unmetalled lanes or a mere track over open grass.

The main interest of that track is the study of how a prehistoric means of communication arises in our climate and type of soil. The so-called "Pilgrims' Way" is the model from which we can study the various causes which moulded the prehistoric road in Britain.

Our remote ancestors, in travelling from one point to another, followed, of course, the necessary conditions applicable to all travel. They tried to make the line as short as possible, subject to other advantages or necessities more pressing. They sought to avoid as much as possible steep gradients, and where a range of hills was to be crossed they sought for the lowest pass compatible with fairly direct advance; but apart from these general considerations, which hold to-day as much as they did then, there were other conditions which primitive man sought when he was making his way from place to place, and which to-day are less obvious.

First, a dry soil. To-day we take this for granted because we have metalled roads everywhere for our main traffic, but men in their beginnings knew nothing of such things. A long way round on dry soil was preferable to a short-cut over damp soil; for damp soil in such a climate as ours makes travel difficult according to its degree of dampness, and marsh prohibits travel altogether. Marsh cuts off travel much more effectively than water. It was the one insuperable obstacle for man save where he was able with great labour to build a causeway. And even in a comparatively high state of development, he will not be at the pains of a causeway save for short stretches.

Secondly, he must in such a climate as ours seek for a track unencumbered by vegetation, and undergrowth in particular. The rough tangle of bush and tree which spreads over half the land in our country when it is left wild is a consideration second only to marsh in the obstacle it presents to travel. One can cut through it; but the cutting has to be continually renewed and the way tended if it is to be kept open. But continual attention to work upon roads was just what primitive society was unable to maintain except where the road was very widely and constantly in use. There was no central government able to compel local communities to keep a road in good repair, and though it might be to the advantage of one particular small district to see to the section of the road that passed through it, no continuous care could be maintained. The early roads therefore avoided brushwood and undergrowth and forest as much as possible.

Thirdly, the early road would skirt areas of primitive cultivation rather than pass through them. Land cleared for cultivation or already naturally adapted to it was too precious to be wasted on means of communication, which could be established in the neighbourhood without trespassing upon the ploughed field. Therefore it is that you so often find an old road going along the edges of an area of arable land rather than passing through it. Fourthly, there remains the obstacle of water. Streams will have to be crossed, and according to the method of traffic used, the crossing-places will have to be of this or that kind.

Let us see how these four points were dealt with in the old road between Winchester and Canterbury; that is, between the populated parts of southern and western England and the chief point of departure for the Continent across the Straits of Dover.

As to good going underfoot (that is, in our climate, dry soil), England was and is remarkable for a great system of chalk which served as the highway for half the communication of the south and east. Very long ridges of chalk radiate like the spokes of a wheel from the high bare country of Salisbury Plain westward, eastward, and north-eastward.

Now, of all soils chalk is the one which keeps the best going for man and beast in all weathers. It can of course get puddled in very wet weather by troops of animals, especially of sheep, whose small hooves churn it up badly; but even then it dries quickly and normally. The chalk with its short grass is good going in all weathers, however wet. Moreover, the chalk formations of south and east England run, as a rule, in high ridges which have a natural drainage. The early Englishman therefore took to the chalk whenever he could as his natural highway, and in this case it carried him nearly all the way from his rallying-point in the south and west to Canterbury, commanding the Straits of Dover.

There was a break in the line, first in the valley of the Wey from Alton, where he had to go on gravel; then later between Farnham and Guildford on sand; but sand is also good going in all weathers, at any rate in this country, where we have no great stretches of it friable and loose. After this stretch of sand, when he had got on to the east side of the Wey at Shalford, the traveller followed the chalk continuously until the neighbourhood of Canterbury itself. He kept, of course, to the southern side of the hills, which was drier than the northern; and save for going every now and then to the summit in order to avoid very steep slopes, he carried on, as a rule, about half-way up, between the plains at the foot and the ridge top.

We should remark in connection with this use of chalk that the prehistoric trackways of England following this soil have the advantage of being well recorded. Chalk takes an imprint of travel or any other form of human interference, such as fortification, and keeps it more permanently than any other kind of soil. Rock is more permanent indeed, but rock does not take the imprint of travel as chalk does, and we owe it to the chalk that we can trace, not only the Pilgrims' Way but the Icknield Way, and many another prehistoric track in south and east England.

As to keeping to open country, free from undergrowth and wood, the chalk again here fulfilled its purpose. Chalk carries beech woods in patches and scattered yew and thorn, but it is not a soil upon which any dense undergrowth arises. Whoever first established this track from west to east may have had some little clearing to do on the sand, and must have had a great deal of cutting to get through here and there in the Wey valley below Alton, but most of the track was cleared for him by the nature of the geological formation over which he passed. It was a coincidence which must have been valuable to the traffic and commerce of men that the natural line from these gathering-places in north Hampshire and Wiltshire to the Straits of Dover should have been so direct.

In the same way the chalk, where it was thus used, naturally indicated the limit of cultivation, and by following it sufficiently high up the slope one was safe from interfering with the ploughed land. For the arable layer of humus gets thinner as one rises on the chalk, and you will trace the Pilgrims' Way everywhere, during all the last eastern part of it, just higher than the culti-vated land, which lies south and below the traveller as he pro-ceeds towards the Straits.

The last point, the crossing of water, is of especial interest in the case of this road. At first sight one would say that in seeking to cross water man in his simplest condition would naturally look for a ford; and one would expect a very old road like this one, the Pilgrims' Way, to cross water, when it had to do so, by a ford. But we think like that because we are so used to wheeled vehicles and animals trained to carry burdens, forgetting what the problem was for unaided man, seeking his way without these advantages. Men can swim, or at the worst he can push himself forward on a floating piece of wood chosen for the purpose, and so cross a river without risk or difficulty even though it be too deep for him to ford. But he needs in order to cross it thus two conditions. First, the place where he crosses must have good, firm ground on either bank; even a short stretch of marshy ground would be fatal to his progress. Secondly he must have a crossing-place where the current is not too rapid; for unless the current is slow he cannot calculate his crossing.

It is interesting to find that whenever this old road has to cross water of any width these are the conditions which it chooses. Later, of course, the bridge and ford were used and a detour made for them, save where a ferry was established at the original crossing; but my point is that the *original* line was not tied to fords. Sometimes the place of crossing happens also to be a ford, a passage where the water is shallow enough to allow man to cross on foot and where the bottom of the river is hard enough to let him cross without danger; but the ford was not a necessity to him. Man never went out of his way to find one in the first establishment of an aboriginal track. The rivers he had to cross between the western centres and Canterbury were the Itchen (where it is no more than a small stream), the Wey, the Mole, the Darent, and the Medway. He had also to cross the Stour, at the very entry into Canterbury. Now, in all these cases you will find that he looked out for a hard place on either shore as his first requisite, coupled with a reach in which the current was not strong. In the case of the Itchen the problem was simple; the stream was small and shallow, and not of a volume or speed which would impede him. It is remarkable in the case of the Wey that he could by some detour have crossed where it was smaller and easier to pass than at the place he chose; but he preferred to take the shorter road, combined with a very good place for taking off and landing, just above Shalford. The steep height on which the ruins of St. Catherine's Chapel now stand has a firm bit of ground at its foot, and there is equally firm ground just opposite, and the broad stream in between is a stretch of slow current.

When our ancestor came to crossing the Mole he had greater difficulty, for the Mole is very muddy, and its banks along much of its course here are soft, and were, of course, softer and more marshy under early conditions. It is interesting to see the way in which the old road here just below Dorking (about a quarter of a mile below the railway station) follows eastward a spur from the Downs until it touches the bank of the water at a point exactly opposite another hard landing-place, the end of another small spur, facing it. The men who established this early track picked out the best point to be found for a mile or two up and down on this small but difficult river.

It is much the same way with the Darent. With the Medway they had to deal with tide, which complicated matters, and the crossing-place has been subject to so much later building and drainage that it is not very easy to judge what it can have been like in early times. It was possibly a place where the early traveller halted until he could get slack water, though anyhow the tide is of no great strength here. The crossing of the Stour just on entering Canterbury presented the same problem; there was a tide, in those days stronger than it is now and reaching far above the place where it now ceases; and the nature of the bank as it then was is lost under at least two thousand years and possibly more of human building and hardening.

After the Stour there were no more obstacles to consider. A man making for the Straits had his choice of crossings; he could start the Channel crossing from the mouth of the Wensum (now dry land) where Richborough stood; or from Deal beach; or from the harbour of Dover; or from Lympne; and to each of these a track led from the central point on the banks of the Stour, the "Hub of the Wheel," where Canterbury came to be built.

The whole length of the Pilgrims' Way has all manner of interest besides these geographical points. Prehistoric stone monuments stood upon it, the last and most important of which is Kit's Coty House, on the eastern side of the Medway. And the trace of the road marks one place after another when events are recorded. It must have been along this way that Ethelwulf marched with the Wessex army to meet the invading Danes who were coming down the Roman road from London, for a little way to the left of where the two roads cross is the battlefield of Ockley, where he defeated them. The banks of the Darent were another battlefield between the English and the Danes, due to the same junction of the old track and the approach to the north, in this case the water approach to the river. And at the very end of the way, rather more than a mile outside Canterbury, right on the track, you may still trace the ditch and ramparts where was fought the first recorded battle on English soil—the fight between Julius Cæsar and the native army on Bigberry Hill.

XVII

The Truce

[Written midway between the two world wars for Armistice Day 1929, this survey and forecast preceded by some years the advent of Nazi rule in Germany and the consequent warnings of Churchill.]

WE celebrate the Armistice, not the Peace. We do well. No peace was concluded when the Great War came to an end; and the reason no peace was concluded was that the powers which, in a sort of alliance, had between them ended the great siege of Central Europe, did not all desire a complete victory: quite half of those powers, national and financial, desired to frustrate the end for which the young men had died.

Therefore was victory not achieved politically, after having been so crushingly achieved militarily.

Those who had been under siege, the Central Powers, were superior to those who besieged them; they were superior in numbers, in unity of command, in unity of field of operations, in morale. They were immensely superior in material.

On the one side stood the German Reich and its Ally, the Austo-Hungarian Empire, the forces of the latter virtually commanded by the former. To them were soon added Bulgaria, the Turkish Empire, the control of the Dardanelles. They had for sympathizers the Scandinavian North, which rendered the Baltic unapproachable. There was perhaps not one educated man in a hundred, throughout the Powers of Central Europe, who doubted a rapid and complete victory. Of one thing they stood in some slight anxiety, the great numbers and the stoicism of the Russian people. Their numbers were patent; what they would endure in the service of their race and sacred dynasty history had shown; but, on the other hand, the Central Powers knew that these great Russian masses were very ill-equipped and that if the vanguard of them did not make good in the first few weeks, their defeat was certain. To the west the Central Powers had against them nothing but the French, debased by a lifetime of increasingly corrupt Parliamentary government, their army harassed by that sort of politician who hates the soldier's spirit as he hates all noble things. The professional politician feels instinctively that nobility is an atmosphere he cannot breathe and in which he would stifle to death.

The French Army was blind. Its Intelligence Department had been destroyed by the politicians after the Dreyfus case. They had wiped out that Intelligence Department, and put the work of the Second Bureau (which until the Dreyfus case had been to the French Army what its Intelligence Department was to the British Navy) into the hands of one of their own civilian corrupt Departments. The French Army had no instrument left whereby to discover the form and nature of the attack they were to suffer. The Prussian General Staff laboured under no such handicap. No Parliamentarians, no Masonic venom against religion, had weakened, let alone destroyed, their acquaintance with enemy plans.

As a result of this contrast, all the first days of the war were an overwhelmingly successful sweep of invading armies through Belgium and the north-east of France.

By every calculation their victory should have been complete. It was bungled; but the bungling was not all on their side. The Marne, which might have been a decisive French victory, was no more than a denial of an expected German victory.

Then came what is called "The Race to the Sea." The Prussian General Staff lost that as they had lost the initiative at the Marne, and for the same reason: lack of "go." They had no excuse. They had better railways and they were working on interior lines; but though they were working with more method, they were working with less energy, and they lost the race. They were contained and the great siege had begun.

Such a siege history had never yet seen, and (I fancy) will never see again. The much more powerful force was contained by the less powerful. The force with indefinitely more munitions was contained by the force with indefinitely less.

It could not long have been so contained, however, but for the increasing weight of England, the gradual increase of English munitions, and, more important still, the prevention by English sea-power of the turning of the siege-line.

But on one side of the containment, the eastern one, the superiority of the besieged was manifest from the outset. The command of the Dardanelles and the closing of the Baltic made it impossible for the industrial activity of the west to supply Russia. On that side the siege at last was raised. But the effect was not decisive because there was no outlet.

Upon the west it was very nearly raised on four separate occasions, and, though Italy had long joined the Allies, the issue hung doubtful. Had not America joined the Allies, the submarine attack on the supplies of England would have decided the issue; and later, when Russia had failed, the Western Front was broken on the Izonzo, before St. Quentin, and on the Chemin des Dames. Yet was the siege not raised. On July 14th, 1918, the last main attack of the besieged to effect a decisive sortie was checked; on July 16th their siege-line was broken in its turn. From that moment it no longer stood but fluctuated. On August 8th the first great hammer-blow was delivered by the British through the northern section of the siege-line; and thence onwards the besiegers pressed forward, taking defensive organization after defensive organization in a fashion which, though upon a far vaster scale, exactly resembled the capture of outwork, ditch, escarpment, final street-barricade, in the older wars.

By the first days of November 1918, the besieged had fallen into complete disarray. They were in full rout; and such as could still speak for them surrendered at discretion, without capitulation and without terms. They were at the mercy of the besiegers.

But the besiegers had diverse objects. The chief financial

powers amongst them, the international bankers of Paris, London, and New York (of Berlin and Frankfort, too, for that matter) were determined to save the Reich, and they saved it. The common religious feeling which creates a natural bond between London, New York, and Berlin, added to the division. Italy was still under its detestable old Parliamentary government of professional politicians, and was treated with a contempt for which we are now paying the price. She had had as many men killed as we. She was not allowed any fruit of victory save a small area to assure the obvious frontier of the Alps; not a colony, not a mile of the eastern Adriatic coast. Even Fiume was shamefully to have been taken from her, and was only recovered by aroused Italian anger at the injustice.

To these forces, ruining what might have been a just resettlement of Europe, must be added the anti-clerical machinery of Paris and Rome. Through the French Freemasons especially, and the anti-clerical school of which they were the core, a Catholic Danubian State and a Catholic Rhenish State were forbidden to come into existence. Anti-Catholic Prussia was reinstated on the Rhine, Bavaria cut off from Austria. Of the new nationalities erected after the Armistice, only one was really favoured, that of Bohemia and the adjacent territories (called Czecho-Slovakia) —and this because the Government of Prague was violently and crudely anti-Catholic.

To refuse the resurrection of Poland was impossible; but it was determined to put every obstacle in Poland's way, because Poland represented the Catholic culture of Eastern Europe and also because industrial finance had no belief in the Polish power of organizing industrialism on the newly enfranchised territory. Danzig, the natural port of Poland, was cut off (out of that evil good came in the creation of Gdynia), and from that day to this there has been a ceaseless assault upon Polish claims—and even the continuous suggestion that Poland should be cut off from the sea altogether and that a great body of Catholic Polish citizens should once more be subjected to Protestant Prussian rule.

Against the Catholic culture in general, even where it is half ruined as in France, even where it is represented by a small nation as in Belgium, half those who fought as Allies in the Great War are now arrayed as enemies. They may mask the position clumsily by vague humanitarian talk (always in favour of Berlin), but that is the position, and all Europe knows it.

What accident may come, or whether any may come, to save us, we cannot tell; because no man can see the future. But this much is certain—that to-day we are not in a state of peace. We live in an armed truce. It is a truce the peril of which gets greater with every day that passes and with every hypocritical phrase used in lip-service to order without justice, amidst such despised absurdities as the annual hotch-potch at Geneva. That truce will either end in renewed war, as is the way of truces, or in a real solution. But this last will never come till men learn to tell the truth, to call things by their right names, to speak openly of hidden power: and that they will do so in time to stave off disaster is, by present indications, doubtful indeed.

XVIII

On Spelling

WHAT fun our posterity will have with our ridiculous worship of spelling!

It has not lasted very long. There has not really been such a thing as spelling for much more than two hundred years in English, and there was no religion of it till perhaps a hundred years ago. Even as it is, the two classes which have most tradition in them—the aristocrats and the workers on the land—care least about it.

I myself write as one emancipated. Time was when I trembled at the thought of a misspelt word, and a blunder of my own or the printer's would keep me awake at night; but now that I have recognized it for the least part of scholarship, and, indeed, hardly a part of scholarship at all, I care for it less than a doit—whatever that may be.

English of all languages ought to be most indifferent to spelling, for upon spelling the sense of its words and phrases hardly ever depends. It is not so with Latin, it is not even so with French, but it is so with English. Here and there you have an ambiguity, as in "affect" and "effect," but, by and large, it does not really count.

I suppose the passion for exact uniformity in spelling goes with all that modern attention to things anyone can do, things that demand no intelligence, things mechanical and of a pattern. It is fostered, of course, by the State educational machine and by the enormous extension of mere print, but its root must lie in the passion for mechanical simplicity and for things in which that man will most advance who is least able to think. It goes with the craze for measurement and with the enormous fatuity that only those things can be known which can be exactly measured, and with that other twin fatuity that when things are measured they are known. It goes with the habit of asking "how broad?", "how high?", "how old?", "how long?", instead of "what is its quality?"

Our fathers cared so little for the ridiculous thing that they did not even spell their own names the same way throughout their lives, and as for common words they seem to have had an instinct which I cannot but applaud for ennobling them with repetitions of letters and flourishes, with the pretty trick of using a "y" for an "i" and doubling consonants. In general, they were all for festooning and decorating, which is a very honest and noble taste. When they said of a man "I esteem hym ne moore than a pygge," one knows what they meant and one feels their contempt vibrating. Put into the present stereotyped form, it would far less affect, or effect, us.

And talking of "stereotyped," there, if you like, is an example of modern spelling! What do you suppose King Henry, the Eighth of that name, would have made of it? But for the matter of that, how little any of those men who made the English language (and I put Cranmer at the head of them) would have tolerated our immense rubbish-heap of long words, not one in fifty of which we know the true meaning of? I suppose that in words ending with "logy" alone there are enough to equal all the vocabulary of the aforesaid Cranmer. There must be hundreds upon hundreds; and by the custom of our time anyone may make up new words ending in "logy" at will with none to chasten him.

Spelling is a great breeder of hatred among the nations, and of divisions, misapprehensions, wars—or as our fathers more splendidly put it (to a toll of drums) "Warres"; as also of "Dissencyons" and "Broils." Here myself I confess to the weakness; to see "labour" spelt "labor" makes me see red. It makes all that is ancient in England see red; and the more openly we admit it the better for international and domestic peace.

Now that this word "labor" should be so abhorrent to the

intimate taste of the English mind is a very good reply to the pedants who will defend spelling as a reminder of the origin of words. "Labor" is right. "Labour" is a twisted thing, coming round by way of a dead French usage. You may say, of course, if you like, that even so, it teaches you a little history and that at least such spelling reminds you that the gentry were French before they were English. But if you say this you lie; for it teaches people nothing of the sort, and such few people as hear this truth about the English gentry only fall into a passion and disbelieve it.

Again, who when he comes across a little word "ink" considers that imperial liquid which only the Basileus on his Constantinopolitan throne could use for his most awful signature? If there is one word the spelling of which ought to teach every child the whole story of Europe and of the great Byzantine centre thereof, it is the little word "ink"—and it teaches nothing at all. Neither, for that matter, does Constantinopolitan, hard as it is to spell.

No, all that talk of spelling teaching one the past of words and things is nonsense. If there was any sense in it we should spell the Canon of a Cathedral after the same way in which we spell a gun. They are the same word; and yet I suppose there is not one man in twenty thousand who would not ridicule the spelling of the Piece with one "n" and of the Ecclesiastic with two. For my part, if I had to give the extra "n" to either I should give it to the cleric, as one of God's creatures and a hierarch and therefore infinitely nobler than a piece of brute metal.

Spelling also panders to the vices of men, and more particularly to social pride. Many a man has lost his soul by putting a redundant "e" at the end of his name to borrow a false rank therefrom. I could quote you the case of at least one peer whose father actually had the name of his titular village misspelt on the map in order to make himself look mediæval. So it is with the people who use two little f's instead of one big F at the beginning of their surnames. They are ffools. In the same way men with foreign names, if those names are of a common sort, will respell them into English; but if they are of the nobler kind it is the other way about—they will turn them from plain English into something Frenchified so as to look as though they were descended, not from tripe-sellers, as they are indeed, but from great barons of the thirteenth century. Thus a man called Roach because one of his forebears had a fish-face, will call himself "de la Roche"; or a man called Lemon because his forebear was too yellow, will call himself "L'Hémon," which is ridiculous. And such men often tell one of two lies: they either say they are descended from Huguenots or are from the Channel Islands.

And all this reminds me that one of the surest ways of insulting a man without risk is to misspell his name. The reason of this (the "psychology" of it, as people say who like to show they can spell) is that every man thinks his name of importance to the whole world, and either known to the whole world or deserving so to be known. It is a very fine example of vanity. For, after all, if the usurpers out of Carnarvonshire remained indifferent (as they did) to being spelt Tydder, Tydr, Tyddr, Tuder, or Tudor, why should we, below the rank of kings, make a fuss about it?

Spell, therefore, at your own sweet will. I not only give you leave of charter so to do, but will at call support you with argument. Only I warn you of one thing: if you do, you are in for lifelong war with the printers, and they are a powerful and close corporation. For now forty years have I attempted most firmly to fix and root the right phrase "an historian" into the noblest pages of English, but the bastard "a historian" is still fighting hard for his miserable life and may yet survive.

XIX

Sardinia

THE island of Sardinia has this great interest, that it is by far the least known, the least generally visited, the least described and written about, of all the Mediterranean lands. And attached to this is a curious point very well worth noting, which is, that Sardinia, almost alone of Mediterranean lands, has kept out of history. It has not produced one outstanding name, it has not been the theatre of one campaign of first-class importance, it has hardly been struggled for even between the rising and falling masters of the Italian seas—Greek, Roman, Carthaginian, Mohammedan, Spanish. Its harbours have formed no bases for great naval efforts; no great work in verse or prose is connected with it; nor even any acute political problem of the present or the past.

Why this should be so it is puzzling to guess. Most people would answer, "malaria"; but there was no malaria there in antiquity, that we know of, and the amount of it in modern times, so far as Sardinia is concerned, has never been such as to paralyse the island. It affects only certain areas, and it is declining. Further, districts heavily affected by malaria have played among the greatest parts in history, and are the subject of perpetual travel, of historical interest, and visitation.

The whole life of Frederick II, the whole story of the Norman kingdoms, in the two Sicilies, the late history of the Greek colonies in south Italy, the struggle there against the Mohammedan, and a mass of other districts in the Balkan peninsula and Greece, would be covered by the same formula, if malaria accounted for the isolation of Sardinia; and there would have been no history of Apulia.

Sardinia, moreover, is rich. It has great stretches of fertile land,

and from the earliest times it has been famous for its masses of minerals. They are still exploited upon a large scale. Yet Sardinia stands thus isolated to-day, as it has been in the past. That is its charm and its delight.

It is a very beautiful country, and the simplicity and happiness of its inhabitants are married to that beauty. Great mountains guard it on either side of the central plain against the sea; it is fairly well wooded, far greener and more welcoming than the French or Spanish coasts, or the Balearics, or the burnt hills of Africa.

Though history has dealt with it so strangely, Sardinia has not been neglected. It has never been allowed to fall into barbarism. The devastating effects of the Mohammedan conquest worked here no such havoc as it did elsewhere, for they were local and passing. The Mohammedans, like other masters of the Mediterranean in history, seemed to think it not worth their while to delay upon Sardinia; and this contempt of theirs has been wholly for the island's good.

Such Christian governments as have successively claimed authority over it have acted well—notably those of the last 150 years, and particularly Charles Albert of Savoy at the beginning of the nineteenth century. Though its country towns are few and small, they are solid and interesting, each with considerable monuments and rivalling in their simple way the sister cities of the Italian mainland.

As for Cagliari, the capital and the main port, it is one of the most delightful cities I have ever come across, both from the nature of its inhabitants and from their traditions, as well as from the very noble buildings which give it such dignity. Above the lower town around the port, there hangs on a high rock the Citadel with its two huge Genoese towers—the Tower of the Elephant and the Twin Tower of St. Pancras. There also is the Cathedral, with its superb marble lions, and, acting as a portal to the steep and conspicuous hill, a great monumental arch and wide stone stairways leading up to a platform, whence one overlooks the whole bay and the surrounding mountains—a magnificent sight.

Unfortunately very few people come in by Cagliari. Other than officials and soldiers, only rare natives returning, and (more rarely still) passengers of the foreign sort, make this fine hill-harbour dominating the southern sea. The boat for Cagliari starts from Tunis; it is an easy passage, fairly rapid and very comfortable, but though it runs only once a week, there is no risk of crowding. When I last crossed, there were perhaps not a dozen people on board. The regular connection with the Italian mainland and civilization in general is by the Bay of Terra Nova in the north, opposite Civita Vecchia, to which there is a good service of a few hours every night, getting one to Rome by the morning.

But that is not the right way to get into Sardinia, for you land in an ill-populated and barren port. The real life of the island lies to the south, or else to the north and east of Terra Nova.

The roads are rare but reasonably good; there is one main railway (with one branch to it) from north to south; and—what I would particularly recommend to anyone who delights in the forgotten places of the earth, though I myself have missed it— many miles of light railway, narrow gauge, threading in and out of the hills, amidst scenery as fine as that of the Apennines lying behind Naples—which is saying a great deal.

The people are of a kind with regard to whom one does not feel that they are "preserved" or "still simple"—a kind that is permanent. What one feels about them is that they never will change; that they will permanently resist the degradation of modern things, and will permanently maintain their sense of grace and beauty. Thus their costumes, the special head-dress of the men and the women, and the ornaments of the clothing are what they have been for generations; and, even in so small an area, these vary from district to district. I came upon one place there where the women wore little bells upon their sleeves, and everywhere one saw the curious Phrygian cap upon the heads of the men, with its long dependent "stocking," much as you may see it in the pictures of the Italian fourteenth century.

Another feature of Sardinia, which it has in common with all Italian provinces, but which is specially marked here because the island is one united place apart, is the local patriotism. The Sards are intensely proud of their land, and they have expressed that pride nobly enough throughout the centuries, in monument and inscription. I have rarely been more moved in my post-war visitations of Europe than I was by the memorial for the young men killed between 1915 and the Armistice. It stands in Orestano, of an admirable simplicity, a model of what war memorials should be in this Europe of ours, where most of them are so unworthy; and on it has been graven in Latin, in memory of how well the islanders fought, three words, of which the English is: "It was the Sards who saved the country."

Corsica

CORSICA is singularly different from the other Mediterranean island, Sardinia, with which one connects it in one's mind as on the map; and, considering how many foreigners winter there and how easy are the communications with Italy and France every day, little known. It is, however, better known than Sardinia.

The reason for this lies in part in the scale of the place, in part in the absence of large towns. It is not large enough for exploration and journeying, and it has, to its own great advantage, hitherto forborne to establish anything like the pleasure towns of the Riviera on the nearest coast.

But I fancy there is a better reason still for the comparative isolation of Corsica, and that is its formation. The island is essentially no more than one big mountain group lifted out of the sea, and almost everywhere coming down steeply into the water. The exception is in the belt of plain on the east coast, gradually widening as you get to the centre, near Aleria. But this plain is very sparsely inhabited, and has a reputation of being unhealthy, and is shunned by the few visitors who know the place.

It is possible that, but for the association of Napoleon with the island, it would be even to-day less familiar than any other part of the western Mediterranean except Sardinia.

And yet the place is crammed with interest, and in beauty surpasses anything else of its region. The contrast between the sharp wooded mountain slopes and the intensely blue sea in its deeply indented bays, the jagged sky-line of the ridges, and the presence, at every turn of its paths and roads, of new and unexpected views down the empty glens to the shore, are amazing.

A great part of this effect comes from the mass of the mountain group compared with the total area of the place. It is as though you were to take an area of about the size of New Jersey and pile upon it a huge group of hills, all high, and the extreme summits of which reach nearly nine thousand feet. This and the fantastic fretwork of the coast-line are the most interesting characteristics of Corsica.

It has always seemed to me that Corsica, beyond any other place I know, is fitted to be a small independent realm. Its people are not only quite different from those of the mainland and of the other islands, they are also filled with an intense local patriotism. They are not Italian in feeling (though modern Italians would like to think so, and though their speech is a dialect of Italian—with very many words of its own and a singularly distinct accent); they have a popular mythology or folkelore, traditional among themselves; and a long memory of efforts at local independence. But, oddly enough, these were never aimed at the establishment of a free, self-governing, and independent nation. They were all as a protest against misgovernment, or alien influence on the part of some continental power, or efforts to attach the island to some other rival power which, it was thought by the evolutionists, would leave the islanders to their customs undisturbed.

Thus the story of Corsica in the later Middle Ages is a most interesting one, not so much of political rising as of economic. It is one of the earliest examples we have of financial power causing an intolerable strain by its subjection of a whole population. The island of Corsica had fallen into the hands of the Bank of Genoa. It was for the Bank of Genoa that the peasants indirectly worked; it was for the Bank of Genoa that the taxes were collected, not directly, of course, but by the Genoese republic; and the people and their leaders came to feel that this alien power was not only draining them of wealth but subjecting them to a sort of slavery. The struggle against that mortgage-hold of mere finance over living people was prolonged through many generations; it was finally successful, but not so much on account of the arms of the Corsicans, as because the economic decline of Genoa had set in.

It is a curious example of how lasting artificial arrangements may be in Europe, that Corsica should be now, upon the whole, better contented under French rule than it had been under any other régime in the last thousand years. It is more than under French rule: it is in political theory a part of France; it is a regular French Department, with prefecture, sub-prefectures, a French organization of the communes, and of taxation, and a system of administration indistinguishable from any other Department of the Republic. There is none of that local differentiation which you get, for instance, in English shires since the war. The school system, for instance, is simply the ordinary French elementary school system, with teachers sent down by the central government, and with exactly the same curriculum, in the same language, as you may find in Picardy or Auvergne.

But Corsica has never felt this as an alien strain, and that is perhaps in great measure due to the special favour shown them by the Napoleonic tradition of the First Empire, and in the middle of the nineteenth century. This tradition established, not in political theory but in social practice, a favoured regimen for the island. Corsica provided the bulk of the police force, its conscripts served, as a rule, under easy conditions; there was less bureaucratic interference with the native habits of land tenure, language, and corporate life than elsewhere.

One very striking example of this favoured situation is to be found in the relations between the Government and the Church. Corsica is as religious as Italy, which is saying a great deal, but one never hears there of those violent antagonisms between the lay state and the clerical organization which had been the curse of the Third Republic upon the mainland.

This is probably due to the fact that there is in Corsica no tradition of French royalism. The French hold on Corsica was oddly acquired by purchase. The government of Louis XV simply paid a sum of money to the Republic of Genoa for its sovereign rights over the island, acquiring them by no right of conquest, with no military decision on Corsican soil either against local or against Genoese troops. That the acquisition was not normal was proved by Paoli's insurrection. What with the short space of time between the purchase and the insurrection, what with the coming of the French Revolution immediately after, no tradition of sentiment arose for the French Crown. Then, in the next twenty years the island shared the glory of its most illustrious son, and was content to be Napoleon's island. It was this, the effect of the Revolutionary Napoleonic wars, which consolidated the present state of affairs. Will it last?

The answer to that question depends, like the answer to so many French problems, on the degree of folly to which the French parliament may go. In times past that institution blundered in almost every department in which it could blunder. It gravely compromised the French position in Alsace and Lorraine, it allowed a revolutionary party to arise in all the great towns, it destroyed French naval power, and weakened as far as it could the French military power. Hitherto it has left Corsica alone. If it continues to do so, all will be well.

XXI

The Witness to Abstract Truth

[An address given at the More Memorial Exhibition in July 1929, before the martyr's canonization.]

I COME to speak to you to-day upon the Blessed Thomas More, and I come to speak of him under one aspect alone; for what one man can say in the few brief moments of a public address should not, upon such a subject, touch more than one aspect, lest his audience be confused. But that aspect is surely the chief one in connection with such a name.

I come to speak to you of the nature of his sacrifice; not of his life, its scholarship, its humour, its worldly greatness, his voluntary decline therefrom; the affection which he gave and received; the multiple humanity which has endeared him to those who least understand his last and tremendous act. For we all must remember that it has become the fashion among those who least comprehend or least love the Catholic Church to make certain exceptions in her favour, inverted scapegoats as it were, and to cite in history one or two Catholics out of the great host of martyrs and confessors and doctors and plain saints, let alone of common Catholic men and women, whom they deign to praise; there is St. Francis of Assisi, because he was fond of animals; there is (for some of them) St. Bernard, because he stopped a riot against money-lenders; and there is the Blessed Thomas More —because when you are praising Cranmer, Henry his master, and for all I know, Thomas Cromwell himself, you must have some counterweight in order to look liberal and broadminded. And the Blessed Thomas More is there ready to hand.

Now all that, I confess, I despise as it deserves to be despised; nor am I here to speak of those other excellences in him which *we* deservedly praise, and for the right motives—his love of justice and of the poor, his contempt of wealth, his self-discipline in life, his merry bearing of the burden of this world—but only the fashion in which he left it.

What I am here to-day to emphasize is this—the Blessed Thomas More died in the support of *one* particular isolated truth, because it was the naked truth, and for no other reason. He did not make a sacrifice of this or that—he had made plenty of sacrifices—he did not give up, as heroic men give up around us day by day, position and income and the comfort of those who are dearest to them for the general Faith. He gave up life itself, deliberately; he accepted a violent death as of a criminal, not even for the Faith as a whole but on *one* particular small point of doctrine—to wit, the supremacy of the See of Peter.

Now let me discuss the magnitude of this act. It is of sufficient greatness that it was performed for one isolated point of truth. But there was much more. It was a sacrifice not supported.

This it is that I desire to affirm, to reaffirm, to repeat, and to repeat again. This is that to which I desire to bear witness, and which, had I the power, I would make prominent in every history. Not that this unique man gave up much for his conscience; that, to the honour of mankind, myriads have done and will do. Not even that he gave up life itself in that cause. Not even that he gave it up for one detached article out of so many. But rather that he found it in him so to act without support: a triumph of the will.

Now consider how men are supported in their rare heroisms.

There is in the first place the support of those who, weaker than the martyr himself, wish him well; those for whom he is a symbol, and who turn to him secretly as a flag-bearer, and by whom they hope perhaps to be later reconciled with that which they know to be the truth, but which they have not the courage to proclaim. He was not supported by an ambient fashion; he was not even supported, properly speaking, by a tradition, and —the most awful thing of all—he was not supported from within by anything more than that supreme instrument of action, the Catholic Will.

Newman said very well that we all die alone; but this is to die alone indeed! To allow oneself to be killed, of one's own choice, in full life, rather than to pay the price of yielding upon one dry, narrow, intellectual point; having to applaud one and to support one and to sustain one neither enthusiasm within nor the sense of agreement from others without.

Let me put before you those two points. They are essential to an understanding of the scale upon which the martyr acted.

First, I say, he was not supported from within.

He had no enthusiasm for the Papacy; he had fashioned for himself no tradition of defending it; no habit, no formed body of argument and action in its favour. He did not defend the Papacy (in a day when its rights were everywhere doubted) because it was second nature to him. No: just the other way.

All his life he had been—as, indeed, was every man of intelligence, judgment, and heart, in the turning-point between the Middle Ages and the Modern—a reformer in the full sense of that word. He had been in his youth the English Erasmus, denouncing with contempt, as did a thousand others, not only the manifold and crying abuses into which the clerical organization had fallen, but many things which were not abuses at all, rather honest devotions, if a little exaggerated. His enthusiasm, the flame of his thought, his memories of sharp emotion in those affairs were all in tune with that flame of reforming zeal, which can so easily in such a moment be deflected into rebellion against the unity of Christendom. About this particular point of Papal Supremacy he had never worried. He had come out of a generation profoundly shaken in the matter; its intellectuals, contemptuous of the state into which the See of Rome had fallen, full of memories of the Schism and of the Councils, far from admiring the temporal pomp and what was worse, the mechanical revenues of the Papal Court. Had Thomas More's death been a death for the Real Presence of Our Lord in the Sacrament of the Altar, for the Most Holy Mother of God, for the golden light which is thrown across the earth by the movement of the wings of the Faith, it would have been quite another matter. He would have been engaged, and the whole man would have been at work. So has it been with great troops of martyrs. But not with him.

He had in this matter of the Supremacy closely examined the thing, as one might any other historical problem: "reading it up" and thinking out the pros and cons. And at one moment— a man of very grave reading, an excellent lawyer, with a brain like a razor for separating one category from another— he had hesitated whether the supremacy of the Pope over Christendom were man-made or not. He had inclined to think it a man-made thing. When he had thrashed the whole thing out fully and thoroughly, he came to his conclusion, as might a judge, without "affection," without any particular movement of the heart. The Supremacy of Peter and of his successors (he decided) was of divine origin.

So far so good. That one point being isolated—intellectual, not moral, in no way attached to the heart, nothing that could inflame a man—he kept it carefully segregated and clear. He was willing to admit the succession of Anne's child; to take oaths of loyalty of any degree and in any respect, save that one point of the Supremacy. And did he run out to defend it with warmth? Far from it! He kept it in the background; he tried not to answer upon it; he followed the debates as might a counsel for the defence, making his points, reserving action.

All that is very cold and very disappointing. But he died— which is more than you and I would have done. And he died merrily.

Nor was this extraordinary man supported from without. I am not sure that such support is not of even greater value (though I admit that the idea is paradoxical) than support from within. Many a man and woman, I fancy, have died martyrs or have suffered some lesser inconvenience after having within their own hearts and intelligences suffered grievous assaults against the Faith, but consoled by the ambient atmosphere of Christendom. "I may through my own fault and negligence have lost my firm hold upon the Faith, but it is my duty to support others who are in better case. They all agree. They regard me as their standard bearer; and I will not yield." Such martyrs, I fancy, will have a very high place; for to serve the faith by an act of will is greater than to serve it without interruption from any human frailty. But at any rate Thomas More was not of this sort. He was not supported from without.

After four hundred years we have to-day forgotten how the matter looked to the men of the early sixteenth century. The average Englishman had little concern with the quarrel between the Crown and Rome. It did not touch his life. The Mass went on just the same and all the splendour of religion; the monasteries were still in being everywhere, there was no interruption whatsoever. Most of the great bodies—all the bishops except Fisher—had yielded. They had not yielded with great reluctance but as a matter of course. Here and there had been protests, and two particular monastic bodies had burst, as it were into flame. But that was exceptional. To the ordinary man of that day, anyone, especially a highly placed official, who stood out against the King's policy was a crank.

We must firmly seize that or we do not understand the period at all. Kings had quarrelled with Popes over and over again. In the matter of doctrine and practice Henry was particularly devout, and strenuously Catholic. Kings had been reconciled with Popes over and over again. For generations the King of England had in practice been absolute master of his realm, and in ninety-nine cases out of a hundred papal action was but a formality. It would be bad enough to make oneself unpopular and to stand out and to look a fool in defence of one particular point of definition—which, after all, might have no meaning a few years hence, when Anne Boleyn should be dead, perhaps, and the two parties to the quarrel reconciled again. That was the point of view (among other millions) of the Blessed Thomas

More's wife, and he was very much what is called a family man, tolerant of nagging. That was the point of view of pretty well all his friends. And it was the more difficult to resist because they loved him and desired to save him. Had they united in chorus to say, "This strong man is standing out; would we were of the same metal!" it would have been a support. But that was not their attitude at all. Their attitude was rather, "This imaginative and highly strung man, who has done more than one silly thing in his time, who threw away his great position as Chancellor and who in his youth published a Socialist sort of book, is doing it again! You never know what he will do next! Really, he is such a good fellow that somebody ought to argue him out of the nonsense!"

No. He was not supported from without.

Let me end by saying that he was not to be supported by posterity. There are men who can repose under the strain of an ordeal in the conviction that their suffering is a seed for the future. I will confess to the superstition that men like More have, in my judgment, some confused vision of the future. If he had, he must have known that his sacrifice was apparently in vain. Could he return to this earth to-day (and I am sure that it must be the least of his desires!), he would not find that he had sown a seed. He would not find—I do not say that he had saved the Faith in this country—even that the Faith had retained such a hold on English life as a reasonable man might have hoped for in 1535. Should the Blessed Thomas More return to life in this, his own country, to-day he would find the Faith an alien thing and himself praised as what I have called a "scapegoat the other way round," a "scapegoat à rebours," an exception which must be praised in order to give the more elbow-room for praising the vile spirits who served the court. At all this he would smile, being a man of humour; or more probably does now smile. At any rate, he has not the support of posterity.

If ever a man died alone, he died alone.

And the moral is clear. It is our business to give up all for whatever is truth, whether it appeals to our emotion or not; whether we have others with us or not; whether our mood concurs or repels. The intelligence is absolute in its own sphere. Intelligence commands us to accept the truth, and for the truth a man must lay down his life.

Let all those, therefore, who in defining the truth, though it be but in one corner and with regard to one arid thing, to them seeming dead, invoke the patronage of this very national Englishman. His fun, his courage, his scholarship will be of advantage to them; so also will his sanctity—if in such days as these I may speak of such a quality.

XXII

The Modern Man

LEST my title should mislead I will restrict it by definition.

I write—not of contemporary man in his infinite variety nor even of the modern European, but of the modern man under industrial capitalism: man as he has been formed through long association with industrial capitalism and particularly as he has been so formed in Great Britain—but not in Ireland save in the industrialist north-east corner of that island.

I write of modern man as you see him to-day not only in the streets of London, Birmingham, Middlesbrough, and Glasgow and the rest, but in the villages; for the whole of our state has by this time arrived at much the same type of citizen (if citizen he can be called). The countryman has become a townee: to put it more elegantly, he has "acquired the urban mind."

So defined, the modern man would seem to have three characteristics:

First, he has lost the old doctrinal position on transcendental things which was that of his immediate ancestry and of which the relics continued nearly to our own time.

Second, as a consequence of this he has lost his economic freedom and, indeed, the very conception of it.

Third, there has been produced in him, by this loss of economic freedom, coupled with the loss of the old religious doctrines, an interior conception of himself which moulds all his actions.

Let us develop these three characteristics and see how they are worked up to make the subject of our inquiry: the individual unit of the modern English state.

With all those of my own generation (I am in my sixty-sixth year) I knew extremely well an older generation which was in all ranks of society fixed upon certain transcendental doctrines chosen out of the original body of Christian doctrine inherited from the conversion of the Roman Empire and its development in the Middle Ages. Though England had been changed in its religious attitude by the great spiritual revolution of the sixteenth and seventeenth centuries and was positively a Protestant country (as she still is negatively a Protestant country), those ancient doctrines which *were* retained were strongly and, I repeat, always universally held. They included the doctrine of free-will; the doctrine of immortality of the soul; the doctrine of the Incarnation, that is, the doctrine that God had become Man, which gave to the personality of man an infinite value since it was so regarded by its Creator; and the doctrine of eternal reward and punishment. There was also retained a certain code declaring what was right and what was wrong; for instance, if you had a wife still living it was wrong to marry another wife. It was wrong to take away another man's property in order to advantage yourself. It was wrong for a public man to take a bribe or to blackmail, and so forth.

It may be objected by some that the old religious doctrines have been retained into our own day. No: not by the average man as doctrines, that is as certitudes. Some part has been retained, but not the same parts by the mass of men. You will still find a minority attached to one or the other of these doctrines. There is a large body which still holds to the doctrine of immortality divorced from the conception of eternal punishment for wrong-doing—and, indeed, from any punishment other than that suffered in this life.

The doctrine of the Incarnation has gone by the board. You may count up a large number of men and women who still maintain it, but most of these are in the minority—a small minority, of educated men, at least—outside the Catholic body. Most of them, moreover (outside the Catholic body), hold it as an opinion, not as a certitude; moreover, they give to it, each of them, any interpretation they choose, while the masses round them have stopped thinking of the Incarnation altogether, let alone holding it even as an opinion. What does remain of it is a sort of vague aroma which suggests that a supposed individual "Christ" who may or may not have really existed, and who is, anyhow, long dead, provides an excellent model for conduct. This model "Christ" is again a figment of the individual's imagination supported occasionally by his fragmentary recollection of ancient documents in themselves fragmentary.

The doctrine of free-will, though inseparable from practical action, has been battered down. The conception of inevitable tendencies, of an inevitable chain of cause and effect, has superseded it. The code of right and wrong has gone, too, and with it, necessarily, the conception of eternal reward and eternal punishment.

Since a man must worship something, there has been substituted for his ancient worship the worship of the community of which he is a member. There has arisen a new religion which is not exactly the worship of the state but the worship of the collective body (formerly called England, now quite commonly called "the Empire"), of which the individual is a member.

That this new worship is vigorous and real may be proved by the test of sacrifice: that which a man worships is that for which he will sacrifice not only his goods but, in extreme cases, his life. The modern man in millions has accepted that sacrifice. The new worship has about it all the appurtenances of a religion in their excess as well as in their normal form—ritual, myth, symbolism.

You may deny any one of the old doctrines and few will be shocked, but you may not ridicule the Flag or the Crown, nor interrupt the Two Minutes Silence on Armistice Day; and men carry in their minds symbols, often externalized in the shape of a map or of a picture, representing this "England" or "Britain" or "Empire" which is the object of their worship.

Now as to the second point, the political consequence of this change in religion: it may be more difficult to persuade the reader that there is here a connection between the cause and effect. For with the loss of his old religion the modern man has also lost the obvious truth that a culture is based upon the philosophy it holds. Yet that truth does remain an obvious truth. If you believe in the transcendent importance and permanence of personality (that is, the immortality of the soul), and in the supreme sanctions attaching to a particular code of morals (that is, Heaven and Hell), you act more or less accordingly. By which it is not meant that the ideal is reached or even maintained, but that it remains an ideal and, therefore, permeates society. Thus, a man to-day most evil in other respects will not betray his own country nor deny the validity of its laws, though he will deny the divine authority lying behind those conceptions.

As to the third characteristic, which is the most practically important for our analysis, the effect of all these on the modern man's conception of himself, it has by this time become glaringly apparent.

We note in the first place that with a loss of the sense of free-will the modern man has lost the sense of economic freedom. We note that temporal good has taken the place of other values. We note that the old moral code, which affirmed property as a *right*—not as a mere institution—has disappeared.

The profound truth contained in the phrase "they that take the sword shall perish by the sword" is nowhere more clearly apparent than here. Temporal good means in practice wealth; and the pursuit of wealth as an end, and as almost the only end, has resulted in the destruction of all those safeguards whereby the individual wealth of the many was guaranteed. As a consequence there has arisen, through the action of unlimited competition, a polity in which a few control the means of production and the many have become wage-slaves under those few. Whether the few who control the means of production will form a stable class or no may be debated. In the immediate past and on into our own day the pursuit of wealth as the supreme good has made the wealth of even the most wealthy unstable.

But there are signs that this state of affairs is ending, and that the strongest of those who control the means of production are creating an organization which will render their domination permanent.

A test of all this may be discovered in the conception of "success." That idea is now almost wholly confined to the attainment of a position among those who control the means of production and are to that extent secure.

The derivatives of this strong attitude of mind are as clear as the attitude itself; for instance, in my own trade of writing, success does not consist in writing well but in commanding large sums of money through one's writing. Another derivative more profound in its effect is the sacramental feeling attaching to, *not* great wealth, *not* lumps of money, but the *possession* thereof. It has become difficult or impossible for the modern man to dissociate the conception of virtue and greatness from the possession of much wealth.

But the most practically important derivative of this attitude is the acceptation by the great mass of modern men of a quasi-servile position. The modern man demands, and is at peace in, the regular enjoyment of payments doled out to him by his economic masters at regular intervals—usually at the interval of one week. He is not controlled in his actions by the fear of any ultimate spiritual effect of his actions, but of their effect upon the likelihood of his maintaining or losing this livelihood. He has no objection to plutocracy—still less to its main instrument, a parliamentary system, the special mark of which is the destroying of direct popular action by the pretence of representation. The modern man is astonished to hear that others regard a king or even a despot or aristocracy as representative of the community; but he is willing to submit to the illusion that an assembly of professional politicians is in some mystical way a mirror of his own will. Though they impose upon him (through the orders of their own financial masters or through their own private interests as rich men) laws which he has never demanded and which he even detests, he accepts the myth that he is only obeying laws he himself has made.

Now it should be clear to anyone who will think lucidly and coldly upon the direction in which all this must move that it is moving towards the re-establishment of slavery. Industrial capitalism, as we now have it, the control of the means of production, distribution, and exchange (and the control of the modes therefore by which production, distribution, and exchange are conducted) by a few, must mean that the many are compelled to work for the profit of the few. When this state of affairs has produced insufficiency and insecurity, the obvious remedies, if we proceed upon the line of least resistance, would be found in giving to the dispossessed (who have come to form the vast majority of those who were formerly economically free) security and sufficiency on condition that they work under the orders of the few. To be compelled to work not at your own initiative but at the initiative of another is the definition of slavery. Whether slavery shall come first in the form of slavery to the state before it arrive at the final and natural and stable form of slavery to individuals—slavery it still is, and the modern man accepts such slavery in the unshakable belief that it is in the nature of things.

Propose to him economic freedom (which can only co-exist with private property well distributed) and he will tell you that the system is impossible, giving as his reasons all manner of external conditions (such as the rapidity of communication, the concentration of the banking system, the cost of great units of machinery), but having for his real reason the mere experience of his life. He has never known economic freedom. He has not seen it in action; and without experience of a thing, one cannot make a mental image of it.

Now, the main political interest of this state of affairs, the political attitude of the modern man, his conception of himself as a unit in society and his conception of society as a whole, lies not so much in the fact that the modern man is heading for slavery as in the fact that he is heading for the consequent decline of our civilization.

That consequence can only come by degrees, even if the degrees be rapid in their succession.

In the first flush of any social system when it has reached its term and its perfection, it works smoothly as a machine and gives high results. One sees that not only in the economic but in the political sphere. When political action by public meeting and debate has been transformed into the rule of one man, that rule works at first more efficiently than did the state of things before the change. Men always welcome the temporary relief of a change which has displaced a thing grown old and fallen out of gear. A properly organized Servile State, the units of which pursue their activities under carefully considered control imposed upon them, would provide a new security and a new sufficiency pleasing enough after the insecurity and destitution of the old broken-down social machinery inherited from days of freedom; but there attach to servile conditions certain characters which eventually lead to the progressive lowering of that efficiency which at first it not only promised but realized.

With the loss of multiple choice in the individual you arrive, to begin with, at uniformity.

The loss of multiplicity involves sooner or later the death of artistic choice. It also involves sooner or later the lowering of energy. Social energy is a function of the zest for living. Under uniformity, imposed and controlled, the zest for living declines or disappears. If this is true of material activity, it is still more true of spiritual activity. Anyone may know how the modern man accepts universal statements even when they are flatly contradictory to his own experience. Any man may note by looking round him how this or that object is proposed for hatred or for affection and then—since there is no spontaneity in the emotion —a contradictory object may be imposed in place of the first: and so on indefinitely.

Modern man has in the short space of half a lifetime expressed a mass of hatred for old President Kruger, for the very ineffectual former Emperor of Germany, for the judges of Captain Dreyfus in the French Army. He may, by the time these words appear, have been stuffed with a similar mass hatred of the head of the Spanish State.

It is customary to ascribe to the influence of the Press the cause of this development, but that is putting the cart before the horse. The Press in its present degradation (and though it may seem impossible to-day, the Press will probably get worse) is but a function of the modern mind. The Press reacts upon the public mind which creates it, as every effect reacts upon its cause, but the chain of cause and effect is not first the Press and then the mentality of the modern urban reader thereof, it is first the modern urban reader thereof with his modern mind and then the Press which is consonant with such material.

The few who have perceived these truths, the few who can contrast the modern man with his ancestry, know that the remedy can only be found in a change of philosophy; that is, of religion. They know, further, that the prime condition which would foster the change would be the reinstitution of private property and its extension to a determining number of the community. But those who see this are, I repeat, few. It is their duty to work upon the lines which their knowledge of the trouble suggests; but it is also their duty not to deceive themselves upon the conditions of their task. It is their duty to realize that this task has become exceedingly difficult of achievement, that the difficulty is increasing, and that therefore they must bear themselves as must all those who attempt a creative effort at reform: that is, as sufferers who will probably fail.

XXIII

On I Know Not What

When I am dead, I hope it may be said:
"His sins were scarlet, but his books were read."

THIS great poem, the noble expression of an exalted but disappointed spirit, was written in the year 1917, and is as true to-day as in that distant epoch when it fell from the pen of genius. For though men are careless of the salvation of their souls (I touch with but the tip of my wing upon *that*), they are all of them anxious, I think, to be remembered after death. And this is particularly true of the writing men, in whom I include the writing women—a far more numerous tribe. For, as the bishop said, or rather wrote, to the parish priest when he put the question about Ash Wednesday: "Beast that you are! Do you not understand that the term 'man' embraces the term 'woman'?"

Here you tell me (and how justly!) that you do not understand the allusion. I will explain it.

There was a custom in the old days of superstition, especially in the degraded countries of the Mediterranean, to observe a season called Lent, and this season began upon a Wednesday. It was a season of fasting, mortification, and annoyance, during which the superstitious and misguided herd, turning their eyes from the delicious prospects of this our mortal life, considered the blank horizons of death. They put aside all memory of mortal sweets, of the toothache, of insults, of misunderstandings, of insomnia, of indigestions, of bills, and of all the other things that go with the pride of life. They set themselves to an examination of that which I am told cannot be examined—for did not a certain Frenchman say that one could no more look steadily at death than at the sun? And was he not right?

At any rate they used, I say, to observe this season called Lent which began upon a Wednesday, and on this Wednesday they were accustomed to crowd to the altar, there to receive upon their foreheads from the thumb of a priest the ashen mark of a cross. And as they received it the priest recited the words "Remember, man, thou art but dust, and unto dust thou shalt return."

Such were their customs. It is related, however, in the chronicles of that time (a little before the taking of Constantinople and a little after the Council of Florence—with which days you are familiar) that a parish priest of the Apennines was in the custom of so marking with ashes upon the forehead the few men that might approach the altar, but not one of the women. For did not the liturgy clearly indicate that it was men only who returned to dust, whereas women, the exemplars of immortal brightness, suffered no such fate? Upon hearing this, his bishop (and there is no lack of bishops in Italy) wrote to him that message I have already quoted, and set things right.

I have by this time, you will observe, wandered somewhat from my subject. But then, what was my subject? If you know you are wiser than I! What I had intended it to be I know well enough. I had intended it to be a disquisition upon the strange love of posthumous fame which is to be found in all the human race, and particularly in the miserable breed of writers. But really the subject has been done to death. I have myself written upon it recently in at least five places, and for all I know in these very pages. And when you come to think of it there is nothing new to be said about it. You all know the main points; they are obvious enough. We shall not enjoy posthumous fame. It hardly ever lasts. When it does, it is usually false. And anyhow, what is fame? You cannot eat it, and under copyright laws your descendants can even make money out of it. So much for that.

But though we know all about posthumous fame, it is great fun looking at it, turning it over in the hand, examining its flaws, and ridiculing it. It is great fun to do this because we who do it are perfectly safe. Even those of us destined to be famous, through the wrongful acquirement of a vast fortune or in some other fashion, are actually alive, and therefore as yet untouched by it. And as it is not one chance in several hundred thousand that we shall have any posthumous fame we may go to work with a free heart.

The first thing I notice about posthumous fame is that it is not more than a label. Of the ten million families inhabiting this island, perhaps one million have heard the name of Milton. And those who have heard of Milton will also have heard of *Paradise Lost*—though not all of them. And of these a fraction will tell you *Paradise Lost* was a very fine poem, and they will praise Milton for having written it.

There they would be wrong, for he did not write it. He dictated it, and this, by the way, is much the easiest form of getting through one's work. It makes one a little verbose, no doubt, and it makes one wander from the point—if one has a point. It dilutes style. It weakens the muscles of the mind. There is everything to be said against it. Nevertheless, if you must write, do not write but dictate. I speak from experience. I know what I am saying. Moreover, a great deal of very good work has been dictated. It would seem that the Romans dictated. Even their poets did so, and we know that Cicero did. Of course you may not admire the writings, or rather the dictations, of Cicero. It is much more probable that if you do admire them you have no acquaintance with them. But I am not engaged (if I remember right) with the subject of dictation, but with something else, which I find upon looking back is posthumous fame, or, at any rate, the thoughts which it suggests. And now I remember, I think we were dealing with Milton, whom some have called unjustly a "crabbed windbag," but of whom Dryden, a very good judge and a very good writer, said: "The old man has done better than us all"—or words to that effect.

I say "words to that effect." There is no more pestilent, prudish, jejune habit than looking up quotations. It interrupts the flow and it is perfectly useless. You know the sense of what the man said, you even know the rhythm of what he said more or less (if you have a good ear), and that ought to be enough for you. Any fool can be accurate with a book of reference at his elbow, but it takes a scholar to know so many quotations that he makes mistakes in every one of them—and I proceed.

Of the remaining fragment, then, that remembers Milton for his *Paradise Lost*, how many have read it? How many have read even a fraction of it? I have read not only *Paradise Lost* several times but, what is more, *Paradise Regained*, and I say without hesitation that the latter is a bad poem and the former an exceedingly good one. But the general fame of Milton is the fame of a label. It is a repeated fame. It is nothing more.

Then there is also this about posthumous fame: that it is oddly ill-deserved. A very comic thing it is to notice the difference between the thing praised, as it stands in the mind of the public praiser, and as it is in itself. I know very well that there are sundry Germans who will tell me that one never can see the thing in itself, because the mind does not transcend phenomena, but I trust that they have learned their lesson.

Also, posthumous fame gets attached to the wrong being. Who wrote *Vathek*? Beckford, you say. At least you answer "Beckford" if you are one of the very few people who have heard of *Vathek*, and at the same time one of the still fewer people who do remember the name of its reputed author. But what proof have you that Beckford wrote *Vathek* in its present form? If I remember rightly, it was originally written in French, and then, if we are to believe him, translated into English by a clergyman. How much had the clergyman to do with it, and how much Beckford?

I may be quite wrong in this, and though I have been saying so braggingly that accuracy in quotation does not matter, I am all in a tremble and in a sweat lest I should here be talking nonsense. So I will take another example where I am more sure of my ground, for I have not read the history of *Vathek*, these ten years—though I have reread the book itself several times a year for at least fifteen. It is a glory.

I will take, then, the *Itinerary of Robert of Cirencester*. For more than the lifetime of a man that book was as famous as a book can be. Gibbon took it for granted, and so did every historian I can call to mind, except a very few who doubted, but did not deny. Then came the exposure. It was quite clearly proved within our own times that the document was false. It was no more an original list of Roman places and roads in Britain than I am. It was made up by an Englishman in Denmark, who successfully palmed it off upon the learned. But there is more in the matter. One is not even certain that the *Itinerary of Robert of Cirencester* was a mere forgery. I think, for my part, that there must have been something behind it. Roads which it mentioned and which were unknown when it appeared have been discovered since its appearance. The very misspelling of names is a powerful argument. I can conceive that the forger, prompted by one of those twisted motives which affect such men, rather than produce genuine fragments which he really had before him, preferred the concocting of a complete piece to the more modest editing of these few realities.

And what else is there about posthumous fame? There is its circumscription in space. Homer is famous enough with us, but not with the Chinese; and, if you will believe me, the French know little of Keats and too much of Byron, and the English are singularly innocent of Lope de Vega. There are even dead men very famous in Wales whom no one has ever heard of in Herefordshire.

On the whole it is better to let the thing go. It will do us no good anyhow, and hankering after it can do nothing but harm.

After all, the great mass of men whom you may see walking down Piccadilly on a fine day are not concerned with posthumous fame, even that of others, let alone of themselves. And I have noticed this singular and illuminating thing: those who have made great fortunes are very nearly always indifferent to so slight, intangible, and airy a thing as renown after death. They also suffer from folly and illusion in the matter of the time that shall succeed their regretted departure. They also passionately desire (as a rule) that their works should remain after them. And they leave fantastic wills, or found a family, or build monuments. But these very rich men (who should be our models in all things) do not, as a rule, care much for the sort of reputation Catullus still enjoys. And they are right. Cash, says the song, is better than fame or rank.

For that matter, I suppose cash can purchase both. And the only reason that a rich man never pays poor poets to write verse for him and to publish it in his name is, I suppose, that they despise verse as it should be despised.

For what is verse? If it is the verse of antiquity, it does not even rhyme. If it is modern verse, it is prose. The price paid for it by journals is not only abominably low but haphazard. It is not sold by length, like prose and calico. There is no standard that I know of for the sale of verse.

Many years ago, when I was an editor of sorts, there was a man who used to write to me from America. He used to send me typewritten verse. It was very bad. With each poem, stuck on with a little metal clip, was a slip of paper, also typewritten, announcing the price at which he was willing to sell. It used to have such words on it as :"The price of this poem is ten dollars." I always sent them back because he was careful to put in a stamp —an English stamp. That shows he was an honest man and also a prudent man. Had he been a better poet, I think he would have been neither.

Reader—it is old-fashioned to say "Reader," but many polite things are old-fashioned nowadays—readerkin, readerlet, do you not think I have kept to my point reasonably well, considering that at the very beginning of this excursion I had already got off the main road, and was diverting through field paths towards the open heaths of nonsense?

Let it be a model to you, if ever you are driven by misfortune to writing. Remember that you can always keep to the point more or less, and that, on the whole, it is better less than more. For blessedness is in variety of experience, unity of affection. And blessedness is the end of man.

XXIV

First Impressions of the City: a Sequel to
The Path to Rome

I AM writing these lines on the 29th June, the Feast of St. Peter and St. Paul. Of course they will appear only some time later, but it is the date which gives me my subject: for it was upon this same day of the year of 1901 that I walked into Rome and saw the city for the first time.

I had indeed had a glimpse of it from the hills to the north as I passed the summit of the road while the sun was still low; and the first distant glimpse of the city remains strong in the memory, and vivid, for all men who have seen it in this fashion: not from the railway, whence one can never see anything, but from the road. It is not, however, this first glimpse that I want to write of here, but of the impression made by the city after I had entered it: the impression made on one's mind by the first general acquaintance with Rome.

These first impressions of places are valuable documents, because, when a man sees for the first time a place in which he is prepared to be interested and of which he has read and seen pictures, there is almost invariably a strong shock of surprise. The contrast between what he expected and what he finds is very great. The consequence of that shock is that he notices very sharply and intensely and immediately the physical aspects about him. They impress themselves deeply and violently upon his senses, and he can never forget them.

An interest of another kind in the first acquaintance with a famous place is the transformation which the judgment effects in later, more familiar, and continuous contact. The town as it really is when you get to know it well, in depth as well as in surface, as it were, is a different matter from the town which struck you so sharply on the first day of your introduction to it. Yet that primal vision will always be a framework for what you learn later on; and I think you remember the physical aspects of a place better from your first superficial but vivid meeting than you do from a wider and more profound and juster knowledge in later years. It is the same with people, especially with people to whom one grows attached. One never forgets the first meeting.

I propose to set down, therefore, exactly what I felt those twenty-nine years ago to-day, without apologizing for its crudity or obviously false conclusions.

The very first impression I got was that things were smaller in Rome than I had imagined. The legend of magnitude in Rome was founded physically on the contrast between its magnificence and the simplicity of smaller towns hundreds of years ago. To-day we have become accustomed to huge buildings, and we expect larger things than we get from antiquity. But another element in this surprise comes from the fact that famous places with a moral greatness convey, when we read of them, an impression of physical greatness. I have never seen the Parthenon, but I am told it produces an effect of much the same kind. One friend of mine said it was "tiny." I know for myself that I had exactly the same shock when I first saw St. Mark's at Venice.

The next thing that struck me, and struck me very strongly, was the quality of the Travertine stone out of which most monuments were built. My first impression of it was more than one of disappointment. It seemed to me almost squalid. I know why that was. I had seen too many photographs and drawings which left the material to my imagination, and I imagined everything to be of marble and to shine. Nowadays my mind so reposes in the Travertine material that I would not change it for the world. It seems to me to be both as dignified as stone can be, and as lovely—two adjectives difficult to combine. Also it connotes for me all that Rome is. But I am setting down a true account, and when I first saw it I thought it tawdry and insufficient.

When I came to the Tiber I was astonished that it seemed to be made of mud. I had expected, I know not why, a stream clear because it was famous. I could hardly distinguish any hills in the city, let alone seven: and the Capitol gave me no impression of height or of steepness. In those days the huge white monument which defines it now was not built. One got the impression of a huddle of houses.

Next I was sharply impressed by the complete contrast between Old Rome, an empty mass of ruins (and comparatively small places built out of ruins) and gardens, with New Rome, built on what had been the exercising ground for the soldiers of the ancient Empire. It was one of those instances in which one appreciates how little maps tell one of a place. I had seen maps of Rome all my life, and because of classical history I had visualized Rome continuous with those times. I was astonished to find that, where had been the fullness of the imperial life, its main palaces, its two chief public places, and all the rest of it, there was now a sort of graveyard of the past, consecrated by monasteries and convents and their gardens.

In connection with that Old Rome but with a part of it which had never fallen into decay, I was enormously moved by the view from the Lateran Gate. There, framed in the gateway, was a splendid vision of the Campagna and the Alban Hills beyond. It is one of the worst changes in the thirty years that have passed since that day that this view has perished. In its place are blocks of new buildings. It is a sort of murder, and ought never to have been allowed.

I was profoundly impressed also with the success of St. Paul's Outside the Walls. Then did I learn for the first time that the Italians alone of modern men can make a modern thing as nobly as their fathers did.

But what I thought most astounding in Rome, almost supernatural, was the singing. I first heard it from the Choir of St. Peter's on that great feast; but the experience did not spoil me for later experiences in other churches. I still think it the most impressive thing I know; and though I have since grown familiar with the next best thing of its kind in Europe, the German church music, notably at Aix, at Linz, and at Vienna, my feeling for the music of Rome is not changed.

Another thing that grew upon me more and more during that first day in Rome was that, in the midst of so much expenditure upon building and statuary and ornament, so little was bad.

I must here explain that this first day in Rome I spent (as is my custom when I enter a new place at morning), alone and wandering about at random, trying to see not as many things as I could, not as many particular or famous objects, but to receive as many impressions as I could. And most of them, as the reader has already discovered, were badly judged, and all of them, being fresh and vivid, were also crude.

Well, then, I was vastly impressed to notice how throughout that peregrination one came upon so little that shocked a reasonable taste. To-day I put that excellent result down to papal government, for I notice that most of the bad was quite recent Masonic stuff, though the statue of Giordano Bruno, a little theatrical, seemed to me impressive enough and dignified. With regard to it I heard a story later which amused me not a little: how that the market women while it was still new to them said, "Oh, look at the good monk!" and laid little bouquets of flowers before it.

Perhaps somebody will ask why I was so specially struck by the excellence of the innumerable Roman details, seeing that I had already known other Italian towns, and that each of them has a wealth of marvels. Well, I still think that no other has anything like such a multiplicity of good work, and, of course, compared with any other large groups of human habitations which I had ever known in the North, Rome was a different world. No doubt the urban centre grouped round the Manchester City Hall, or Birmingham, had at that time a larger population and more separate buildings in which to house it.

Perhaps more money had been spent upon them. But the result was less satisfactory.

The next point in my recollection was this: "Where are the Middle Ages? They seem to have disappeared!" Everything was sixteenth or seventeenth century, with an emphasis on the seventeenth. (By the way, talking of the lateness of the decoration and of exceptions to the excellence in everything, I marvelled greatly at the eccentric tower of the old university, and I wondered who had found it necessary to be so odd. There must have been someone—thought I—who was determined to be novel at all costs. Even in that youth of mine I knew that such an appetite was to be deplored.)

The great history of Rome is mediæval history; but of those tremendous episodes which filled my imagination and of which I had read so much, there seemed nothing outward to guide me. It is said that Sir Walter Scott, when he visited Italy, was impressed by nothing save the bastioned square fabric of Bracciano. The saying may be a joke, or it may be true. I can understand it of any man who loved the northern Middle Ages, for the Castle of Bracciano is one of those great feudal strongholds which you can match throughout France and England. But in Rome I could not find my Middle Ages.

That was partly, of course, because the change to modern times began so much earlier here, partly because the true Gothic North—in the terms of which I interpreted the Middle Ages—was always different from the South, but most of all because the great bulk of expenditure upon Rome was the rebuilding of the city in its churches; at least after the turn of the sixteenth century.

But I should like to put on record this: that much of the seventeenth and eighteenth centuries in statuary, however excellent, seemed to me, in that youth of mine, half dead; and that I was moved as by a vision when I saw that splendid bronze recumbent figure in the Chapel of the Blessed Sacrament in St. Peter's, where the Middle Ages and the Renaissance meet.

That is the test of statuary—to express the multiplicity of the soul. Such a revelation is triumphant throughout the hundreds of figures at Brou; it crops up suddenly, exceptionally, hundreds of years too late, in the work of Houdon; it is profound in the anonymous bust of the widow (somewhere about 1600, they say) in South Kensington: it shines through the faces in Rheims; but the glimpses of it down the centuries are rare. It is an angel's visit.

Of St. Peter's, wherein, as I say, that recumbent figure struck me far more than anything else, what I best remember about the huge church was that I could not grasp the size of it. I had heard all the old tags about the canopy of the high altar being about as high as one of the old Roman palaces: I had curiously noted the lengths of other cathedrals marked upon the pavement. But the only thing that brought the scale of the thing home to me directly was the statue holding the holy water stoup, on the Gospel side of the main doors.

The reason of this was that I at first looked on it from the far side of the building, not noticing the corresponding statue near to where I stood, then, walking over to look at it, it grew upon me like a little mountain. That it represented a child made it look bigger still. It was indeed a monstrous child.

You may laugh at me if you will, I shall not mind. But another thing which impressed me in that enormous hall was the discovery that the mosaic pictures were mosaic. I had thought they were oils. When I found they were made of little bits of stone and would last for ever, I was taken aback. I had always associated mosaic in my mind with an archaic convention. When I saw this full, realistic, late Renaissance form and colour, not on canvas, where I thought it could only be, but in the hard unchanging material of those pictures, I had seen a new thing.

Lastly, in St. Peter's, was I puzzled to come round the corner of a pillar and to see the memorial and the tablet to the Stuart kings. It takes a young man a long time to get rid of the falsehoods he has been taught as I had been taught history at Oxford (if teaching it may be called). I could not yet conceive of the rightful kings of England, in their exile, as being what they were. From that first chance glimpse of that small memorial I began to recover a right perspective.

Let me conclude with two mere affirmations undiscussed and unexplained. The sight of those enormous town walls, uninterrupted, unhidden, centuries upon centuries old, gave me the scale of Rome in the dimension of *time*, as did nothing else, save one other matter; an episode of a day or two later, when I was taking coffee with a friend, and he said, looking at the marble columns of the place where we sat, "They came from the Temple of Veii."

Good Lord! I thought they were common marble columns, such as you find in the cafés of Paris or Brussels; instead of which, it seemed, they dated from the Gods.

XXV

Foch

[Written at the time of the Marshal's death in 1929.]

WITH Foch there passed from us one of the great men of our time. That conclusion reads at first so weak and thin that it seems a waste to set it down. But it needs saying because we live in a day when opportunities for judging scale in human affairs are lacking. The nations do not know one another. The various classes in the nation do not know one another. Public information is in the hands of a tiny group of men whose main business it is to deceive, and who, even if they were honest, have neither the brains nor the instruction to distinguish what is important.

We can only judge of greatness to-day—or of anything else— by direct contact. The old means of judging, cultivated criticism, has disappeared. We can only judge men to-day when we have met them. It was in direct contact that Foch's greatness appeared. It was composed of five things: Judgment, Character, Intelligence, Special Aptitude, and Virtue. Whether greatness can exist in a man without virtue has been argued threadbare. I am inclined to agree with the ancients that it cannot. At least, all the forms of evil which I can list, from indulgence to pride, obviously lessen a man. It may be there is some form that does not. But this is certain, that Virtue, when it is mixed with and illumines talents of a lesser kind, adds at once an element of greatness, and when these talents are eminent, it inspires them and makes them transcendent. Of that native virtue let me give one small instance. One day when he jotted down for me in the Invalides that sketch-map of his position during the Marne which I preserve, I asked him, reverently, to sign it. He looked at me in surprise and said, "Why?" He did not know, it was no part of his mind, that such a record was history or himself a giant.

Those who discuss Foch as a general are apt to miss two points: first, that the late war could not, of its nature, illustrate the genius of generalship in the only form which history knows it—that is, as an individual effort governing all the main outlines of a united action. It was too vast, its development too novel, and the diversity of the Alliance too great for any such display. Secondly, that we must wait at least twenty years—perhaps fifty—before we know what really happened. But it is true that, more than any other one man, Foch won the war. It was his intelligence, his power of co-ordination, and his judgment, but most of all his *character*, that concluded the last phase: a little vanity, a little passion, or a little bewilderment at the end would have lost it. This would not be true of all military actions by any means. Vanity has helped to win some, quarrelsomeness or violent passion others; bewilderment none. But it is true of this war. The combatants were at the last extreme of nervous tension. Their national pride, their physical powers, their social discipline, were all exasperated and but just on this side of sanity. A wrong handling of the United Command, a rubbing-up-the-wrong-way of a colleague, an underrating of troops foreign to the Commander, an illusion either way upon the remaining strength, moral and material, of the enemy would have been fatal. It was providential that in Foch was found that combination of moral qualities which made any one of these errors impossible to him. He never entertained, let alone expressed, that disparagement of troops other than those of his familiar experience, which is the commonest fault of judgment in the soldiers of an alliance. He never quarrelled; and, perhaps most remarkable of all, he gauged with singular accuracy the *degree* of moral strength in the forces opposed to him at any moment in the last four months. He did not gauge it with exact accuracy. Nobody could. He more than once thought a particular result would be less than it was. The judgment of colleagues and subordinates was even often, in such details, happier, for *one* moment and of *one* aspect, than his own. But if one considers the general view the man took from the 12th July to the first days of November 1918, it is singular for its appreciation of how much—or rather within what margins —the enemy resistance would stand.

I think it is true to say also, as I have done, that he never quarrelled. He insisted but he did not challenge. Not that he was of those who avoided conflict of that sort on principle as though acquiescence and smoothness were virtues, but because he understood the moment. He knew—as most did—that a disagreement in the last strain would be fatal. But, more than any other man and in the one position where it was most difficult, he carried that knowledge into action.

In the midst of much ill-fortune—overwhelming misfortune —the Allies had one piece of good fortune quite exceptional, which was the similarity in this excellent feature of Foch and Lord Haig. The two men differed as widely, one may say, as the two nations. And how widely the two nations have come to differ in the last 300 years can only be clear to those who know something of them before the divergence in Religious Culture began. Haig was in every characteristic a man of this society and nation: Foch entirely French. But each had that positive power of handling without friction and that negative power of avoiding excess in mutual relations, coupled with the still rarer power of co-ordinating the work of subordinates, which between them give a commander that character of which I here speak. Moreover, you may find in each that very touchstone of value in these times—a hatred of publicity.

The juxtaposition of two such men under the conditions of modern France and England is extraordinary to the point of the miraculous. It compensated for that mass of ill-fortune of which I have just spoken.

For if ever alliance was weighted down by adverse conditions, it was the alliance of our group. Prussia and her satellites entered the war with a United Command, an effective recruiting field overwhelmingly larger than that opposed to them, a still more overwhelming superiority in material and most important of all—a form of government suited to war. They also had the advantage of surprise, having prepared the attack at long date, and having ordered the first steps of mobilization before any rival. The Alliance, morally fragile and incoherent, which had to meet this formidable superiority, was under Parliamentary Government at its worst; some of our elements were hardly equipped at all, others imperfectly. The intelligence department of the French Army had been destroyed by the Dreyfus Case, and never restored; the first phases of the war were the boxing of a man who can see against a man who has been blinded. Throughout those four years the ridiculous Parliamentarians of France, Italy, and England continued to play their pettifogging game and to strut through their sorry parts and to declaim their third-rate conventional rhetoric as though the world were not at stake and as though they were its natural-born leaders. They interfered with the soldiers and sailors to the very end and secured only one thing; the ruin of the peace. Yet the Alliance was—by the skin of its teeth—victorious. It was victorious because the soldiers and sailors unlike the little twisting clots of politicians, were men of a definite trade, with definite tried aptitudes and with real talents that could be subjected to real tests. And the greatest of them was Foch.

It will be an excellent test of our generation and the next in Europe to see how they preserve the memory of such men as Foch and Mercier. If the decline of our civilization is as rapid as it promises to be, their names will be blurred or even perhaps lost. If they are increased and more sharply defined, we may hope that there is enough critical power left and enough conscience to save Europe.

XXVI

On Preserving English

THOSE who admit that the English tongue is without rival as a vehicle for human expression are concerned for its preservation; and they are not only very numerous, but of the best judgment in their time. The men who so discover the English tongue to be without rival are those who can compare it with others and who have some knowledge of what it has accomplished.

Yet they all feel—I at least have never found an exception, and I am no exception myself—that the machinery for achieving their end is not only lacking but difficult to conceive. In modern times the English polity has taken a turn which makes it difficult to do moral things by strict institution, and the guide or mastery to be erected for the preservation of English is therefore to seek. There seems to be no way in this or in any other matter of the mind but drift; and though we give drift very pretty names, in order to flatter ourselves as drifters, drift will not mend matters.

What we can do in the affair—and it is of no great positive value, but of considerable negative value—is to discover where the chief dangers lie, so as to be warned against them, and not to mistake for dangers what are not dangers at all.

Now the first great danger is a moral one. It consists in abandoning the struggle by saying that change in the language has always been and will always necessarily be, giving examples of it in the past, and even going on to say that, since change is a condition of growth and of life itself, it is useless to combat it—that of their nature things organic cannot be static . . . and so on. This state of mind has all the disadvantages; it is foolish, it is ignorant, it is platitudinous, and it is allied to a similar weakness in many other departments: it proceeds from the spirit which tolerates almost any evil in the State by pretending that such things have always been and that it is waste of energy to attempt their remedy.

It ought to be apparent to any one with an elementary knowledge of letters, or even of life in general, that mere formless change is not the law. The law is one of growth, maturity, and decay. But with those things which we cherish it is our business, upon their arrival at maturity, to arrest their decay, and that this can be done with a language is not only historically certain, but may be said to be the historical rule. Latin crystallized: had it not done so we should not have had for nearly two thousand years a medium for our common culture in the West, and therefor that culture would not have survived. Greek became so set that lyrics in language indistinguishable one from another, and prose which only an expert can separate by periods, stretched from before the age of Pericles until the fall of Constantinople in the fifteenth century. And this is not only true of the great twin classical languages, which are the basis of all European things, but, if scholars may be credited, of almost all other vehicles of almost every other established culture.

The man, then, who despairs of preserving the purity of the English tongue is committing a sort of treason, for he is despairing of preserving the English spirit and that which it has impressed upon the common mind of Europe.

It is some consolation to affirm that one element in conservation is fixed: modern English literature. The slight difference between the English in the later seventeenth century and the English of to-day is not a difference between two dialects. It is, for all effective purpose of culture, inexistent.

It is with the middle of the seventeenth century that what Englishmen now know as England arose: its existing morals and religion, its commercial expansion, its political ideas, and, with all that, its written tongue. Now, that great body of matter cannot be destroyed, and necessarily erects a norm from which it may be difficult to depart. Or rather, from which, if we do depart, and perhaps our posterity will soon depart from it, English letters will lose their power.

The next and lesser enemy of the English tongue is a concentration upon mechanical detail in the effort to preserve it—too great a distaste for neologisms, and (what is to me personally a peculiar irritant) the setting up of pedantic little rules, most of which are false and all of which are unimportant.

You do not preserve the purity of the English tongue, for instance, by carefully going over the sentence you have written and transposing the adverb in a split infinitive. There is nothing un-English about a split infinitive; every cultured man and woman uses the split infinitive all day long, and even in written English it is a tolerable, though it should be a rare, exception. But, at any rate, a split infinitive is always better than a sentence barbarously warped in order to avoid it. It is much better to say, "I want you to understand this clearly" than to say "I want you to clearly understand this." But much worse than either is, "Clearly to understand this you must read so and so." Sentences like that are written by men who have first written naturally with a split infinitive and then taken the wretched word out with a pin and stuck it wriggling in a still less suitable place.

Worse is the habit of laying down not only pedantic rules, but false ones—as, for instance, that an English sentence should never end with a preposition. Why, it is one of the characteristics of English that you can, and very often should, end a sentence with a preposition! It is one of the things that separates it from the languages derived from the Mediterranean only. It is one of the characteristically modern things in the existing and matured tongue.

No, the verbal enemies are other. And I should like, by way of conclusion, to emphasize three of them, for an enemy discovered is half beaten—if you have the power to beat him at all; and in language, corruption comes in through failure to note its advance.

These three main enemies, then, seem to me to be, first, the introduction of foreign phrases and terms which do not meet a want as neologisms do, but which are either redundant or oust the old native phrase. They are evil because, at the best, they lack the local association and tradition which give a tongue its vigour and sap, and, at the worst, jar against all our methods of thought. ("The will to conquer" is English; "The will to victory" might be Choctaw.)

The second is the fatal habit of loose wording: of ambiguity, of using words in one sense and then arguing from them in another; of suspension—that is, using words which are of their nature relative to some end as though they were absolute ("efficient," which by itself means nothing; "able," which by itself means nothing; "faith," which by itself means nothing); of emptiness—that is, using words with the sense washed out of them ("clever," "perfect," "charming").

The third is the neglect of construction—and it is the most ominous as a symptom of decay. It is hardly a lifetime since all writers *attempted* to construct their prose, to give it rhythm and proportion, to "see" a paragraph and a sentence and a phrase, to conform to an architecture. Most succeeded; to-day perhaps half a dozen attempt it. Attempting a rare thing, they succeed—for they would not attempt it if their ears did not feel the acute need. But the public ear feels that need no longer—and that is like the falling of a night.

XXVII

Peace to Israel

SOME years ago, shortly after the War, I wrote a book with the title of *The Jews*. Many of my friends when they heard that I was going to write it begged me to pause before running so fearful a risk—the most dreadful things were going to happen to me if I were to break the taboo. I was to be boycotted, imprisoned, starved, maligned, all sorts of other things all at once. Such is the terror inspired by Israel, and very comic it is to watch its effects.

Then there was another group of advisers, and a good deal larger, who gave me to understand that anyone writing on the Jewish question wrote himself down by so doing as a fool, a crank, or even lunatic. But I knew all about that, so I paid little attention to it.

When you come to think of it, what an extraordinary thing it is that this one interesting public question should, in this one country of England, be treated in so absurd a fashion! Of course there has been a close understanding between our commercial-aristocratic state and the Jews ever since the 17th century; most of our great families have Jewish blood by this time, and it has always been taken for granted that support of the Jews was as much part of patriotism as persecution of the Irish. But even allowing for that, I cannot think that there is any sense in the old taboo of silence. It was not required by decency, nor was it to the advantage of the country. Praise Jews by all means: worship them if you like. But why pretend that they aren't there at all?

Anyhow, I published my book, which bore the motto (in Hebrew) "Peace to Israel," and the thesis of which was very simple and clear. It was to this effect:

There is a grave problem everywhere in the modern world called "The Jewish Problem," and it arises from two facts in combination: one, the fact that a particular race with strongly marked characteristics and a strong feeling of racial solidarity among themselves is spread at large throughout the world; second, the fact that as a rule there is friction between the members of this race and the members of the other races among whom they find themselves.

Here are two facts which you can no more deny than you can deny the Great War, or the sun and the moon. They are perfectly plain truths, and they are important because it is self-evident that between them they create a grave problem. They create a grave problem because there necessarily arises through them a danger of cruel and senseless attacks upon the Jews which do a double harm: they obviously do harm to the Jews themselves, and they lead to widespread and long-enduring antagonism against the people who persecute them.

I said that the principal factor in the problem was the conclusion which the Jews appear to have reached, that their best policy is one of concealment. And it is here that what is special to my thesis came in; for the rest of it consisted simply of plain facts which people elaborately pretended to be non-existent but knew very well to be true. Is it better for the Jews themselves and for the world that this elaborate pretence should be gone through that the Jews are not Jews but Englishmen, or Frenchmen, or Irishmen, or what not? Many people think it *is* better so. In England at that time nearly everybody thought it better; and I think most people think it better even to-day. Now I maintain that on the whole the policy is not a good one, and that it would be a much better thing to base ourselves on truth, to admit the existence of the separate race, give it a special position of its own, and frankly and openly discuss the dangers which beset it and the best way of avoiding them.

It was astonishing to note what a hubbub this simple proposition of well-known truths and of quite clear, though debatable, policy produced. I got masses of letters denouncing me for that kind of lunatic called an anti-Semite. One magistrate in America denounced me in public when I visited the United States ten years ago as a man who ought to be deported, and one of their leading publicists accused me of writing with what he called "a poison pen." I discovered this to mean in the local idiom a piece of writing which says one thing while suggesting another; something like our English proverb, "Don't nail his ears to the post."

Now my thesis may have been right or wrong; there is a great deal to be said against it. It is perfectly true, for instance, that Jews loyally serve through the greater part of their lives the country in which they live and in much the greater part of circumstances act as other citizens do. In fact one may say they always so act except when they feel their own security attacked. It is also true that long habit and association give them a great deal in common with the other races among whom they live. I for one believe that the feeling of affection which they have for their surroundings, though perhaps not as strong as ours, has a considerable strength, and that when they express it, it is genuine. They possibly feel it more strongly for one kind of society than another; but still, there is a sense in which one can say that Disraeli was an Englishman or that the generous Doctor Rothschild is a Frenchman. There is nothing untrue or grotesque in calling one English and the other French. And in the same way one may say that Signor Sonnino was an Italian. Also, it may be argued with great force that conventions involving a proportion of falsehood are often useful and necessary. The convention which prevents, for instance, lese-majesty; the convention which makes us wear clothes; the convention by which we ask sympathetically after the health of people of whom we care not a rap whether they are flourishing or in agony.

But the point about my little book, which I think did a good deal of good in its way, the point which I would recall now, in 1933, was a certain prophecy which it contained. It is unwise to prophesy—and nine times out of ten it is actually silly. It is a habit I have avoided in my writing, because I have always appreciated what a fool a man looked when his prophecy did not come off. Thus, though during the War I wrote millions of words on the operations, I never allowed myself one prophecy of what the future would show, save (I regret to say) the risky one that Bulgaria would be the first to break away from the enemy coalition. I happened to prove right—but I ought to have said that it was probable, not that it was certain.

Now in this matter of the Jews also I did make a prophecy, because it seemed to me so certain that it could be predicted, as one predicates the necessary consequence of observed physical facts. I said that sooner or later there was bound to be an explosion against the Jews in this or that white, western country as yet not to be decided. I said that the 19th-century convention could not be indefinitely maintained, the strain was too great and the lie too enormous: where the crack would come I could not tell, but that it would come somewhere I was pretty certain. All the past was there, to prove the unhappy cycle of the Jews: persecuted in one country, received as welcome immigrants in another where the persecution was denounced, and then in time getting at loggerheads with their new hosts and suffering a new persecution. Indeed it was because this was so obviously the teaching of history that I drew my conclusion, and said that the only way of breaking that wretched cycle of cause and effect was openly admitting their difference and giving the Jews a special position of their own.

Well, the prophecy has come off. The old Hohenzollern prophecy of the Middle Ages is reported to conclude abruptly with the accusation that the Jews would be to blame for the breakdown of the Hohenzollerns and would pay for that act with their lives. *Israel infandum . . . morte piandum.* Whether there really be any such mediæval prophecy I know not, though I have seen the reported printed text of it.

The present trouble is an effect of the Dreyfus case at long range. The new Prussian revolutionaries have access to all the archives: they know what a Jewish agitation may work against a nation and did work against France and the French army; they already ascribed to the Jews the evils Prussia had suffered through her own fault; they feared to suffer as France had suffered, and the result is before us.

I do not think that the way in which the Jews have been treated by Prussia, abominable as it is, will lead to any particularly bad consequences for Prussia itself. I think that if Prussia gets into trouble it will be through her own grotesquely swollen head and her consequent total misunderstanding of her true position among national forces to-day.

But I do think that one important consequence will follow from the abominable actions of these hysterical fools in Protestant Germany. I think that they have brought the Jewish question out into the open, and that it will remain there. In so far as they have done that, good will come out of evil: for I am still convinced, as I was all those years ago, that the conventional falsehood upon the Jewish question, especially as practised in this country, much as there was to be said for it, is bad policy as well as bad morals.

[Written in 1933 during the early days of the persecution by the Nazis whom Belloc refers to above as the new Prussian revolutionaries]

XXVIII

Advice to a Young Man in the Matter of Wine

April 1934.

MY dear Young Man,

You will, for many bad reasons, desire to achieve a reputation in the matter of wine.

If there is a dipsomania in you, so that a glass of claret and water imperils your reason and your life, you will advertise your abhorrence of wine upon moral grounds. This public attitude of yours will, if you are rich, be loudly and widely praised. When you shall have bought you a seat at Westminster, you will speak against the evils of drink and applaud the laws purchased by the liquor monopolists for crowding the refreshment of the public into restricted hours. You will further boast that the accursed stuff never enters your house. Meanwhile your guests of any importance will be given champagne at your table.

If you do not belong to the small but powerful clan of wealthy dipsomaniacs, you will want to be accounted—yes, even in youth—a connoisseur in wine. It is an ambition handed down from more cultured times than ours, and one that still hangs on among the English gentry. It has survived the boast of an acquaintance with the classics which once accompanied it. No gentleman to-day quotes the Odes of Horace, which, indeed, few gentlemen have read and fewer could appreciate; but there is still some respect shown for a man who understands claret.

If you have already travelled on the Continent you will repeat as your own the judgments you have heard others pass on the vintages of Europe. You will recall a wonderful Chambertin of '19, which you will smack your lips at remembering, though all you know of it is from hearing a commercial traveller talking of it at a table next yours in Dijon. You will describe your own delight in that vintage, and embroider upon that lie whatever else occurs to you, though in fact you have not wittingly drunk one glass of it in your life, and would not have discovered its excellence if you had.

Now, no rules can make you a connoisseur—and perhaps there is no such thing as a full judge of wine. But there are three main rules, the observance of which are of life-long value in the *use* of wine, and these I will suggest to you.

The first, the most essential canon, is that wine of every sort, so long as it is pure, must be taken seriously as a chief element in life. It is the concomitant, and perhaps the foundation, of all our culture. "Man without wine is an ox," said the wise man—and he was right. Man without wine is a boor.

The unfortunate nations of the North (before they took to boasting, which has become by this time their chief vice) were eager to learn from the South, and so acquired the arts of building and writing which are now so much imperilled. But most of all did they seek wine. Even the wretched barbarian pirates of the northern seas, whom by the Grace of God we beat off (but with difficulty; Alfred did it here in England upon the Downs above Westbury), sought wine as their first loot when they came to Christian lands. Making a custom of wine, they gradually drank in also manners and an appreciation of truth, goodness, and beauty —all of which languish in the absence of wine.

It is not a matter of fine wines or costly. All wine is of this high function. A wanderer in the Lesser Atlas may get wine plentifully at a penny a bottle—it is the wine of the young lions —but though it is so cheap it carries civilization with it. The unhappy Mohammedans among whom the traveller there finds himself are not familiar with wine. Perhaps if ever they became so they will at last mix with us and make one family, abandoning their errors. It is high time. They were not always thus starved. In the great days of Islam wine was the glory of its captains: *The Arabian Nights* is a witness to that. The Persians still know its virtue. But some four hundred years ago reformers arose in the Moslem world, filled with zeal, and they destroyed the tradition of wine, insisting on the text of the Koran—since which time Islam has drooped and declined.

Note also how the Spartans fell. They added to their other brutish qualities an abstinence from wine. With what result? That they died out and their power was extinguished. Some brief generations after their chief victories they had dwindled to a few hundred men, and soon after none were to be found. They had perished. Nor have they left any memory or monument. Athens, august in the use of wine, is immortal gloriously, but who reads or remembers Lacedaemon? Where are its songs, its visions, its philosophy, its laughter, or its marbles? There are none known, for they had none. Lacking wine, the Spartans could not create, and their city was transformed into a squalid hamlet, which it remains to this day. So much for the Spartans.

But if this first rule be granted, that wine is the fundamental and necessary thing for those who would lead the world, there must be added a second rule, which is this, that wine should never be abused. Drunkenness on wine is a horrid thing. It is a waste of the best in the worst. An excess of wine destroys all good in wine, Nor is there anything easier than to avoid such excess, for true wine, that is the red wine pressed fully from the grape, announces its own satiety. A man needs so much of it and no more—as with bread, which is wine's brother. If a man pass the limit which wine naturally sets upon its own use, he can no longer enjoy it. He does not taste it or know its character. The God has disdainfully withdrawn.

Remark, however, that the limit of sound drinking varies widely from man to man. I knew a man once who was a Burgundian, and a soldier by profession. This man, though from the vineyards, could drink no more than two tin-cupfuls of wine in the canteen. If he drank more he became a wild fellow who would fight his comrades; so that, more than once, I have seen him bound with a forage-rope lest he should do injury; he was thus tightly held, blaspheming, until the fit had passed. But I also knew a great Scotsman who would soberly sip three bottles of his Larose through a winter's evening, supported by his mutton and communing with his fellows (upon theology as a rule) from five o'clock, his ancient dining hour, until ten—a very noble example. For your plain man one bottle of red wine at a meal is a just measure. Indeed, it is thus that the bottle came to be what it is, holding one meal's provision, about one-sixth of a gallon. It is enough—but not too much. It is the very symbol of temperance.

The third rule in the drinking of wine is this: "Drink what you like." "Si placet bibe," as the Abbot (or Abbess) said in that allocution to his (or her) community in the Abbey of Theleme —itself a foundation of the vineyard lands. "Drink what you like"; that is, do not drink wine of this name or of that year for the sound of the name, but go by the taste of your tongue.

I say "of the tongue" and not "of the palate"; for it is not the palate that tastes, but the tongue—and, perhaps, the tonsils: wherefore a curse on them who pull out tonsils or in any other way mutilate our glorious bodies! They have but a short time to gambol in, have our poor bodies: while it lasts, for God's sake let them have their fling—our bodies. And, indeed, there are some (two Deans, one Bishop, and ten Atheist Dons among them) who maintain that we are but bodies. What rubbish! Whoever heard of a body inanimate, uncompanioned by its immortal spirit, writing even tolerable tumpty-tumpty verse— let alone an organ threnody or a Complete Sonnet! (For that matter, you reply, whoever heard of a spirit—mortal or immortal matters not—doing anything whatsoever without a body? I answer, Mrs. Parthwich, of Worthing, saw her brother's spirit very plainly, all dressed in white, phosphorescent, and moaning horribly, and that some five weeks after the old boy's death.)

Drinking, then, as I said, is to go by taste. Never depart from this Third Rule in the matter of wine. Wine is good if it tastes good to you. If it does not, then it is not good wine; and the best wine is merely that which tastes best. There is no other criterion.

You may take a Chambertin of '23, keep it till '38—only four years hence (by which time I take it that this full-bodied stuff will be introducible)—and call it good. But if you maltreat it, if it gets frozen or boiled or corked or jostled or vinegarized, or in any way transmogrified, the magic number '23 will not save it. There is no potency in dead names or numbers where wine is concerned. They show what *may* be, and even what *should* be good; but not what *is* good. Just as a Gangworthy of Thapton should be a gentleman, but may be, from some fault in upbringing, startlingly otherwise.

Go by your taste. At first, in youth, it will tell you little; but it will always tell you something, and as you grow older it will tell you more and more. Never affect to feel a special pleasure in wine that seems to you not remarkable. Never fear to praise no matter what wine, if it really pleases you. Remember the story of the man who, tasting some wine in a friend's house, said: "Where did you get this?" to whom his host answered: "From the grocer round the corner." Whereupon, rising early the next morning, the guest went round to that grocer and bought all there was, before his host had come down to breakfast at ten—his hostess having, as is the custom, breakfasted in bed. He went round the corner, I say, to the grocer at 9.45 a.m. winter time by the meridian of Greenwich (though himself in Kirkcudbrightshire), and bought all there was at 36s. the dozen! It was a Richebourg. Whence came it there? No man knew.

I also once, at Instow, drank a wine of which no one knew the origin, but I think it was from Paradise. Only, there was this about it—no other bottle of its kind was left.

I now end my main rules for the use of wine, insisting especially upon the Third.

For, as to the First, that wine must be taken seriously, all wise young men know that, and the unwise will be taught in this matter, as in all others, by the strict schoolmaster called Time.

As to the Second, that wine must not be abused by excess, it is more difficult to practise. For, though Time also will teach it, a habit of abuse is difficult to eradicate. A wise woman said to me once that if every man, on drinking a trifle too much, got a sudden clout on the side of the head from an invisible hand, there would be no drunkards. But who, of mortals, is to give that clout? Little men are afraid, big men are usually too courteous, and the guardian angels of men are forbidden direct action —worse luck!

Anyhow, if you drink too much you are a fool, and worse. But you will never, *as a habit*, drink too much red wine. It is not red wine that destroys men.

As to the Third Rule, it is, in practice, and for you young men —particularly for you of the rich sort—the most valuable of all. If you never praise but what you enjoy, you shall do well.

It is true that you should listen to the Ancient Drinkers, and when they assure you that such and such a vintage is remarkable, you should attempt to appreciate it by habit. But never say you like when you do not like, or are indifferent.

As a man approaches death he will, if he is wise, recall the happinesses of his life and render thanks. In this list of blessings he will particularly remark the occasions of his coming upon unusual wine: wine of Olympus, or even wine of earthly content—which content can be stretched to an hour. No man can draw up in his mind a list of occasions on which he drank a wine which he had been *told* was good. It must *taste* good to leave any permanent inscription on the heart. It will be of no service to you to go up to the Lord God at your judgment, pulling your forelock and loping your knee, and saying: "Oh, Lord God, here is the list of wines I have been recommended by certain knowledgeable men: the Duke, the Master of St. Beves, the Landlord of the Dragon"—and with that to pull out a roll-call of strange names and dates. No, a man is judged by his heart. And if your heart was not touched, then grandness will avail you nothing. But at your side a humbler little man, coming with a scrap of dirty paper, will say: "Lord God! Here I have written down with the stub of a pencil the name of the place called St.

Alery, where I drank I know not what wine which seemed to me divine; it was under the high but blunt and flattened hills of the Charollais." That man will enter heaven because he told the truth.

Are there no other rules to be given about the use of wines? Millions of them!

Never warm red wine by putting the bottle before the fire or into hot water. This abominable trick turns red wine into vinegar. For that matter there is no reason why you should warm red wine at all: it is good enough cold, even in the coldest weather. But if you are for having it warm, let it take slowly the temperature of the room in which it will be drunk. Stand it in that room four or five hours before the time when you intend to drink it; then, if it be a wine with any body in it, take the cork out half an hour or so before the hour and lay it across the top of the bottle. This piece of ritual has magic in it, and therefore no one can give you the reason for its making the wine taste better—but it does.

Another thing which makes red wine taste better is to baptize it, or rather to baptize the first glass of it. Baptizing means putting in one tiny drip of water and no more. It certainly brings out the flavour of a wine at the first drinking as nothing else does.

As for white wine, you should always cool it. In winter it is usually enough to put it into cold water out of doors, but in summer you should cool it in a jacket of water, as our fathers did—and not in the abominable, truncated and plated-tin cooling pails of the restaurants, which are worse than useless. These cooling-pails are designed to cover about half the bottle, and they were brought in so that the other people in the restaurant could see the gold foil on the top of the bottle and know that you were drinking champagne. The result of using these sham coolers is that the first two glasses at least are warm and spoilt—for the cooler liquid sinks, and if you cool the lower half of the bottle alone, the upper half gets no benefit from it. Our fathers knew this, and therefore made their wine coolers in sections lined with lead, each section big enough to hold a bottle right up to its neck. The best way to cool wine is to have a circular drum (a Bath biscuit tin does very well), which drum must be a little wider across than the bottle is. Stand the bottle in such a tin and pour in water till it almost reaches the cork; then quite a little broken ice floating on the top of the water will rapidly bring the whole of it down to freezing-point. But it is a mistake to cool white wine too much, for it prevents one's tasting it. It is enough to put it in iced water a quarter of an hour or so before drinking.

There is another rule about wine which is not universally true, but worth remembering for general application: the second cheapest wine on a common wine list is usually the best of the cheapest wines there. And here, again, I beg you to remember that neither the year nor the name in itself makes the wine good. Once more I say to you, go by the taste. You might take a Clos Vougeot of '28 (which will, I suppose, some years hence be among the best wines in the world), and by mishandling it— by putting it into a cellar full of hot-water pipes, for instance— you may ruin it so that it is worth nothing.

Do not despise sweet wines. And here, again, go by your taste. When I was a boy, before the Flood, there had already arisen a piece of snobbery (and it is astonishing how wine, like horse-flesh, lends itself to snobbery) which taught men to pretend that taking dry wine showed knowledge of the world, or wealth, or something of that kind, and that liking a sweet wine was undignified, or argued poverty or lack of breeding. All that is nonsense, or, as the poets say, tripe. In certain sorts of wine, for instance the *strong* Spanish and Portuguese wines, the Sicilian wines, and those from volcanic soil such as the admirable wine of Orvieto (which will not travel a mile), sweetness is essential. If you had them dry they would be monstrosities. For my own part, I could never abide dry sherry, even when it was thin; but that is mere personal taste.

Remember that a great number of the wines you come across

will be concoctions, and that some wines, notably port, are necessarily and unavoidably concoctions—that is, they are not the unmixed fermented juice of one grape, but a blend of such and of boiled wine, spirit distilled from the same wine, and other things. There is no harm in the blended wine, and people who understand the value of simple and cheap wine are wise when they blend, for instance, the common vintage of the Herault, or some such, with the strong African stuff. But still, there is no judging a blend, for there is no integrity in a blend. Any wine, to be thoroughly good, must be wine unmixed.

Here is another little rule. Burgundy always tastes better when it is carried over the sea in the wood and bottled in this country rather than when it is imported in glass. Why it should be so I do not know. That is true also in a much less degree of all the red wines, but it is particularly true of burgundies.

I was almost going to end by telling you where to get the best Hermitage of the year '21, but, on the whole, I think I will not.

XXIX

The English Highway

THE English highway has necessarily that in common with the roads of all the West which it owes to the common history of the West. It has its strata of prehistoric tracks, of Roman military communications, of the deflections in the Dark Ages therefrom, of the great mediæval complex renewal and extension, of the first modern attempts at properly engineered roads, of their partial supersession by the railways, of the recent revival through the internal-combustion engine. But the English highway has also certain features peculiar to itself which are an excellent theme for anyone who is seeking to understand the story of England.

England is the island of rivers and of ports. There is no other great island thus intersected by waterways which reach right inland to the very heart of the realm in such multitudes, so easily to be used by men for the interchange of goods and ideas. The other, lesser, great European islands—Cyprus and Crete, Sicily, Corsica, Sardinia, Iceland—have no such system at all. These rivers are served by powerful tides (Reclus, I think it was, who called such tidal rivers, not for the first time, "roads that take you back and forth of themselves"), and they have the peculiarity that they run through the land where most wealth could be produced in the old agricultural time, when the system of highways was founded.

England is also the island of ports, which is not quite the same thing as saying "island of rivers," for many a good port lies at the mouth of an insignificant stream or of none.

Now, a port immediate to a good hinterland is a rare thing. Why, it is hard to say; but so it is. Look at the coasts of Italy, of the French Atlantic seaboard, and observe how a mass of land-wealth may lie subject to insufficient exit. In all the space between Bari and the lagoons of Venice you have nothing but the Hook of Ancona, which is no true natural haven. On all the better provided western coast you have, between Naples and Genoa, but one reasonably large refuge and four small ones if you include the two river mouths of the Arno and the Tiber. All the way from the fine inlet of Brest to the Pyrenees you have but the two Breton shelters, the Hook of Quiberon, the Loire, La Rochelle, the Gironde, and Bayonne. It is curious and difficult to rationalize the way in which harbours are thus chary of serving the land that demands them. You have splendid accommodation all down the Eastern Adriatic and all down the Scandinavian peninsula—with nothing behind it to export or to receive and pay for imports.

When you turn to England the wealth of ports seems extraordinary. I count rapidly along the south coast alone of natural inlets for craft of moderate tonnage (such craft as were universal until quite recent times) a dozen main entries which include the great gulf of Plymouth Sound and the unique land-locked shelter behind the Isle of Wight, and does not include perhaps another dozen of smaller places.

Under those two conditions of river and port the English highway by land was a means of going from port to port by way of bridges over the main rivers, and especially by way of the lowest bridge over the greater tidal rivers, which lowest bridge would be thrown as far up inland as possible (because it was cheaper to take goods in by water than to cart them by road. Thus you have for the chief point of this kind in the island, London Bridge; for another, Gloucester; for another, Chester; for another, Newark; and the great primary roads are determined by them all.

Now add to these conditions three more. One is that through the greater part of the south and middle of the island, where its original wealth and population lay, there are no lofty ranges and little necessity for seeking a pass; next, that the climate is very wet; lastly, that the soil is highly diversified, and is remarkable for the great system of chalk ranges radiating from Salisbury Plain. Put all this together, add the north-central Pennine lump, the high border between the Scotch Lowlands and North England, the single passage to Northern Scotland by the bridge and highly defensible Rock of Stirling, and you have the original skeleton of the English highway system set up.

First, the four great ways of the king, that "St. Andrew's Cross" of which the Romans later made the Watling Street and the Fosse Way; the two main lines, one of which takes you from the ports of the Straits to the port of Chester, the other of which takes you from the ports of the south-west to the estuary of the Humber. They were so laid out as to take the dry water-partings, and each, through the greater part of its length, the one up to Newark, the other as from London Bridge (and before that, perhaps from Lambeth Ford), avoids the crossing of all waterways save in their very highest reaches. Where those two original great ways cross, not far from Leicester, was held to be the very centre of Britain, and I have gone off the main road more than once to look with awe upon the few ruined stones which remain of the monument the Empire set up to mark so sacred a site.

From this great "St. Andrew's Cross" there spread out north-wards the two ways east and west of the Pennines, the one by York, the other by Manchester and Lancaster, each in its turn using the lowest river bridges. Then they converge on Stirling, which is the gate to the Highlands, and so on by paths like veins to the extremes of Caledonia.

London Bridge created a secondary system of its own, a western road to the Severn with a branch to the Mendips, and another down to Winchester and Southampton and Portsmouth harbour; the two roads from the Sussex coast, one from the mouth of the Adur, one from Chichester; and the main road northward from London; the road north-eastward to Colchester and on to the main Norfolk estuary and (I suppose a branch of this) the Pedlar's Way.

It was from this framework that all the rest developed, and in particular the tracks of the Dark Ages and the side-roads which seem to have been hardened in the twelfth and thirteenth centuries (at least, up to then most battles and most great buildings are determined by the older, Roman ordered, main roads; but afterwards appear more and more haphazard).

One accident befell the English highway which stamped it in a form we both suffer and enjoy to this day. That accident was the dispersion of power into local hands and the corresponding depression of the central Crown just at the beginning of our modern era. This political fact it was which crystalled or froze our lesser local roads into a permanent system, narrow and full of twists and turns, even when their use was necessary to pass from one great centre to another. A strong central monarchy would have refounded, as did that of Louis XIV, the old system of Imperial ways: a local aristocracy gave England, among many other things, the English road we know, with its peculiar beauty (already menaced), its narrow frame of hedgerows and of fine trees, its twists and corners delightful to the eye, one of the chief blessings of the old good time gone by, and to-day the thing we know in the toll of accidents.

Yes: the aristocratic system, like every other thing, force, will, or organization of human kind, did good and evil; and here it seems to have done both good and evil. It saved and enhanced the English landscape, it preserved the English village, it married the soil of England to the building of England, so that when you come upon any English county town which is still of moderate limits and of antiquity, upon any English village of the older sort, upon nearly any one of the older country-houses on its slope, seen through its groves, all that you see is part of one thing: and it is a thing the like of which you will find nowhere else in the world.

As for what harm the gentry also did, and whether their

magistracy, their double senate, their fruits in education and all the rest, were good or evil, or a mixture of both, like the tree in Paradise, I may safely leave you to debate that among yourselves; for I will not venture here into the morass of discussion, but remain upon that better thing, the Road.

Gilbert Chesterton

THERE were in the work of Gilbert Chesterton two elements: the thought which it expressed, and the method whereby that thought was expressed. These two elements are present in all work of tongue or of pen, but in the case of Chesterton they were more distinct than in any contemporary: I might almost say more distinct than they are in the work of any other modern writer, English or foreign.

The thought in Chesterton concerned the discovery of reality and the conveyance of that discovery to his fellow-men, or rather to his fellow-citizens—for his effort was essentially national. But the method was of a kind rarely associated with such thought. It was a method of illumination by metaphor, and by what is often called epigram but should more properly be called vivid and isolated phrase. With this method he inter-mingled continual play upon words. As this last character in his prose was the most sharply in contrast with the matter of it, it has attracted the most immediate attention. But the core of his prose is certainly not to be found in this verbal play, but in the exact precision of three things: perception, comparison, and statement—especially comparison.

There, in the baldest form, may be stated the greatness of this great man; and there may we discover, in the matter of his thought and the manner of his expression, what his future effect may be.

I say purposely "effect," not "standing" or "position." For this august friend, now dead, was concerned with his purpose entirely, and in no way concerned with the repetition of his name on the lips of others.

The proofs or examples of his power to perceive reality—not

to attain it by some process but to perceive it—is seen in many forms of what he did and was. Let me enumerate them:

In the first place (and much the greatest example of all), his attitude towards the Catholic Church. He was not of those men who come towards the Faith by a gradual approach wherein the outlines of the city grow clearer with each advance, who first see it dimly without recognition, and only at last are in full possession of its meaning. He was one of those who from the beginning both knew there was something there and knew what it was that was there. What he had to determine, and did determine after a long process of resolution and meditation, was the full value of the claim—not the nature of the Presence. What he himself has said of himself was true indeed: "He could not be anything but Catholic." The final step he took was in the same undeviating line as that which his vision had followed throughout his life.

Now the Catholic Church is the one window through which man may gaze upon reality in what concerns the most important of all things to man—the nature of man and his destiny. One consonant through his very nature with the Faith, one instinctively responding to it before it is acquired in its fullness, is one endowed with a faculty for reality.

Next, I would point out another unexpected but most striking example of this power of perception which was the head of his genius. His drawing of character upon paper. It is more living more real, more the human being itself, than anything called character-drawing by the literary method. More real and more living than any of those found in that art which he himself so intensely admired in the older writers who were the subject of his study and his enthusiasm, He would, with a soft pencil capable of given every gradation in emphasis from the lightest touch to the dead black point and line, set down, in gestures that were like caresses sometime, sometime like commands, sometimes like rapier-thrusts, the whole of what a man or woman was; and he would get the thing down on the paper with the rapidity which only comes from complete possession.

There was no counter-order in his mind as he drew; there was no adumbration; there was no sketchiness or duplication or experiment. It was like a word said in a moment by a voice completely sure of what it had to say. He drew of such human beings and their emotions, even their full characters, presented at once upon paper, hundreds upon hundreds. He produced them with the facility of Nature producing flowers and leaves. He drew these things as a perpetual and necessary fruit of his personal activity; often they were to be reproduced and printed, quite as often they were not. And the mere fragments of that vast production each carry about them *life*.

No one else has done this, even among the few who have attempted to illustrate their own work—as, for instance, did Thackeray; and the unique thing was unique not only through its miraculous exuberance, but through its perception of reality. Generations hence, any man may see our modern money-dealer, our modern English woman of the world, our modern, honest, well-founded merchants (such as remain), our poor, our middle class, our boobies, even, occasionally, our heroes. All our humanity in procession, with the alien type called, I think, "Imperialist"—or so called at least in Gilbert Chesterton's youth and mine. That very characteristic figure—both as cause and effect of modern England—is recurrent through the whole.

Another example of this perception of reality was the joining of metaphor to fact. The application was as absolute as the inlaid work of the old masters in cabinet-making; the illustration fitted exactly into the thing to be illustrated. I know no other such immediate connection of the known and the unknown in English literature; I mean no other such inevitable connection of a familiar instance, exactly explaining an idea misconceived through familiarity or through lack of instruction.

What was true of his power in this regard was true of his concision of phrase, especially in his discovery of motive. And in the examination of any critical point in politics or letters or religion the discovery of motive is the supreme test of perceptive power. When you know why a man has said this or that, you know him and his saying and his presumable effect.

Now, Gilbert Chesterton added to this unique intensity of perception, to this discovery of reality permanently and in a flash, the determination to convey it to his fellow-men. He used for this purpose, as I have said, verbal play to arrest attention (including puns); he used that astonishing power of metaphor and illustration, but much more did he use logic. In exactly the reverse order, from the less important to the more important, did most of his contemporaries in his own place characterize him, giving much the first rank to what mattered least and hardly noticing at all what mattered most. It is a commentary on the time and conditions in which we live that a mind of such calibre should thus be judged at the first impression: luckily it was only the first impression. Second thoughts will be very different, for it is in the nature of the active reason to achieve results that endure.

As to the verbal play of which they make so much, I will beg anyone who reads this to consider that Gilbert Chesterton's mastery of words had another side to it, far more deeply enunciating the man himself. I mean his verse. I need not quote from it to express its quality, as it is sufficiently famous, but I may be allowed to say here (as I have said in many another place) that I think his *Lepanto* is by far the most active and most complete rhetorical poem our generation possesses.

The next article in his method—parallelism, comparison, simile, illustration by the juxtaposition of fact with facts and idea with idea, illumination of a concealed or forgotten truth by showing its mirror-like resemblance to some other well-known and admitted thing—this was an instrument far more characteristic of his work and far more effective than any suggestion through the similarity of words. All his work is filled with the brilliance of this talent.

And here again there has never been anything like it. No one else in English letters had used this kind of argument save with labour and by rare exception. With Gilbert Chesterton it was native, perpetual, and of the strongest effect. I might almost add no one will again do such a thing, and I think that could confidently be said. His own work may set the fashion, but it is a method which, like high lyric verse, must come naturally or be abandoned. And it is native to very few indeed; it is soon abandoned by those—nearly all men—who to find a parallel must explore and commonly end in approximation only.

Concision of phrase, giving the heart of a truth in one epigrammatic and brief collocation of substantive, verb, adjective, was a faculty in him triumphant. He stated in this way a character and the moods that drove it to action. He exposed a confused or a false, still better an inept, phrase. He threw a searchlight upon the dark, shadowy part of assertion which is to-day nine-tenths of the whole. He did all this as no one else could.

But far the first of his actions was his action through logic, through an appeal to the reason. Now it is almost always true of such appeals that their weakness lies in one of two things, they are dry or they are lengthy and tedious. Chesterton short-circuited the tedium and plentifully watered the aridity. The whole thing was both succulent and short; and yet it was a proposition stated and proved.

It is here that we touch upon the grave question, the solemn problem, which we who remain alive for some little while after him will continue to consider, but which only our sons or grandsons will be able to answer. All this profusion of active genius, all this resurrection of reason in a country and in an age which has actually begun to pride itself upon having abandoned reason, may or may not fail in that effect which he himself so ardently desired. Being from beginning to end an effort to establish reality, its success or failure must be measured in the course of the next two generations by the measure of its result in the restoration of the Faith to this country. A thing thus of the future and a thing of such moment cannot immediately be dealt with. It must be put wholly as an interrogation. Time, not our time, will supply the answer.

[An appreciation written at the time of Chesterton's death, this essay was in part developed by *On the Place of Gilbert Chesterton in English Letters*—published in 1940, but now out of print and rarely obtainable second-hand.]

XXXI

Once More

THERE is an elementary truth which has been repeated over and over again in this paper and elsewhere. The repetition must be continued because it is only thus that even obvious truths can be made to pierce in the days through which we are now living. The excuse for repeating it and hammering it in is that the very highest political consequences depend upon its appreciation. That truth may be formularized as follows: "Under capitalism the producer has every motive for *not* producing wealth."

Another defect from which our time suffers is lack of definition. Words are used in all manner of different senses, and to hardly any one of those senses is the exact meaning adapted. In such an atmosphere it is impossible to reason or to analyse without clearly defining the terms one is using.

Let me repeat therefore that definition without which all discussion of these affairs is meaningless: "We mean by capitalism a system under which wealth is produced by a mass of citizens, politically free but dispossessed, and these working for the profit of a far smaller number of effective owners and controllers of the means of production."

It is no objection to this definition that a great number of dispossessed who are occupied in the production of wealth own *something*; they nearly all own the clothes they wear, and most of them own a few sticks of furniture. Great numbers own small units of capital, a few certificates, or a few shares, or a policy: but the governing condition of their lives is that they are working for the profit of other men and, further, are under the inhuman control of those other men.

Now, that word "inhuman" is of first importance. Human servile relations, domestic control, are tolerable things. Mere

mechanical control exercised by anonymous wealth imperson-
ally is not tolerable. It will kill itself and the society which it
governs. Meanwhile it is an increasing plague.

The typical unit of production under modern capitalism is a
factory or a transport system in which citizens of the dispossessed
kind (commonly called proletariat) work at a wage, on the
reception of which at comparatively small intervals depends
their existence. This wage must be less than the total amount
they produce by their labour; that is, there must be a margin of
profit (normally) between the wage paid by the capitalist to the
proletarian worker and the value of what the latter makes: for
if there were no such profit, actual or prospective, there would
be no reason for the capitalist to set the machinery of production
in motion. For instance, if a capitalist body hires ten thousand
men to dig out of the earth a million tons of coal in a given unit
of time, the mine cannot be carried on unless the values received
in that unit of time, as wages by the miners, is worth a good
deal less than the million tons of coal which they have extracted
by their labour from the earth.

Under these conditions of work undertaken for the advantage
of another, it is necessary and self-evident that the less the wage
of the worker the greater the profit to his employer. It is further
necessary and self-evident, that the advantage of the worker is to
do as little work as possible for as much money as possible, and
the advantage of his capitalist master is to give the worker as
little money as possible for doing as much work as possible.
Under such an arrangement the man who actually produces the
wealth must be for ever aiming at producing as little as possible
for the wage he receives. Whatever form the equation takes,
that is the truth which it expresses. The proletarian worker may
be aiming at shorter hours or less pressure during those hours or
for an equal number of hours at a larger wage, but it is all a form
of producing as little as possible.

In whatever way you put it, it always comes to the same
thing. The man who is producing the wealth tends to produce

as little wealth as possible per unit of time. It is of no advantage to him to produce as *much* as possible, it is of every advantage to him to produce as *little* as possible, short of losing the wage upon which he lives. The worker is necessarily out to kill profit, and yet profit is the motive whereby the whole system is kept going!

It is no answer to this clear truth to say that organization and scientific work and all the rest of it bear their part in production quite as much as manual labour or the tending of machines. Of course they do. But vastly the greater part of organization and scientific work and the rest is done at a wage just as much as manual labour or the tending of machines is done at a wage. The man who looks after his own individual business in which he exploits a number of proletarians and successfully directs their labour himself is an exception to-day; and even he, as a rule, in proportion to his success, takes less and less direct action as his life proceeds. The mass of all work, intellectual as well as manual, even in a successful individual business, is proletarian; in company business it is all proletarian.

The direct consequence of this paradoxical state of affairs, in which he who produces wealth is, by every economic motive, driven *not* to produce wealth, is the necessary ultimate breakdown of the whole system. There comes a point after which it cannot carry on, but must, in order that society shall survive, be transformed into one of two alternative types, the one fully servile, the other based on property. Either the mass of the proletarian workers must be compelled to work by force for the profit of others and under the control of wills not their own, or the motive of property must be restored whereby the man who works can profit directly from his own labour.

The intermediate or preliminary stage which may be called "the formative period" of capitalism is a lure. Men who have lived under it, and especially those who have prospered under it were vaguely of a mood that it could last indefinitely. It could not so last, for plain arithmetic forbade its endurance. So long as there was an indefinite supply of unorganized proletarian labour or so long as the proletarian worker inherited the traditions of a better time when his ancestry were possessed of small property, capitalism could expand and flourish. But those conditions were of their nature ephemeral, and they are now passing away so rapidly that the effects of their departure are already threatening the whole body of our civilization.

Attempts to reconcile capitalism and contented industrial labour have in them self-contradiction. They are often called "palliatives," but they are worse than that. They are the attempt, or the pretence, at reconciling contradictories.

We have a very fine example of such folly in the French "Social Laws" as they are called. The hours of labour are shortened by compulsion. The scale of wages is raised by compulsion. What follows? What obviously and necessarily follows under a capitalist system of production is an increase in the cost of production, and therefore in the price the worker himself has to pay for the things he consumes. Finding that the price of these things has risen the worker again organizes to demand a further rise of wages which, if the profit is to be maintained, means a further cost added to the produce—and so on indefinitely.

It is a good thing that this particular "experiment" (as its author called it) has broken down so quickly and so thoroughly, for it has exposed the radical error which vitiates all such policies. You cannot be and not be at the same time. Not even the most muddle-headed fool, enamoured of what he calls "compromise" or "gradualness," can be such an ass as to conceive that being and not being are simultaneously possible. Hard and strenuous work cannot be—cannot exist—at the same time as slack work and little of it. High production of wealth cannot be coincident with low production of wealth.

There are no issues from the situation (whether you call it a vicious circle or a blind alley or whatever metaphor you choose) save servitude or the restoration of property. You may restore property collectively through the guild, the corporation, or individually or by families, where the method of production makes that possible. But if you *don't* restore property, you restore slavery.

You may compel men to work, and the servile compulsion is of the same character and effect whether it is exercised by an individual, a body of individuals, or the State itself; or you may leave a man free from such compulsion and give him citizenship. You cannot do both at the same time. The whole of our civilization has now to make up its mind, and that quickly, whether it will take the road to civic freedom or the road to servitude.

XXXII

Seven Fables from Aunt Æsop

I

THE LAMB AND THE WOLF

A FINE fat Lamb occupied in drinking at a Stream was annoyed to see the Water Muddied by a Wolf which had approached the Further Bank for the same purpose. "I do wish," said the Lamb, "you would not come and Muddy the Water out of which I am drinking! Besides which, why can't you behave yourself properly as we Lambs do? Why don't you first come to the right side of the stream and ask leave to drink and then come at the hour which would be fixed for you? Why can't you be law-abiding like us Lambs? We have no patience with you! We Lambs will never tolerate Disorder or Lawlessness—Remember that! Please go away! We don't interfere in your affairs—don't interfere in ours!"

The Wolf, legitimately Annoyed, thereupon sprang at the Lamb and Ate Him Up.

MORAL: The Meek shall Inherit the Earth.

II

THE LION AND THE MOUSE

A Lion, having the misfortune to be caught in a net, asked a Mouse with bright Eyes and prominent Features (Who happened to be watching Him) whether He would not kindly bite through the Entanglement? "How much?" said the Mouse. The Lion without hesitation answered, "Ten pounds." "Ten pounds nothing!" said the Mouse. "Twenty," returned the Lion, after a short pause. "Nft" (pronounced Nift), was the mouse's reply. In some Agony of Thought and consequent Delay, the Lion was about to say "Thirty," when a Cat appeared, ate the Mouse and was off again. Wherefore did the Lion perish miserably of Hunger and Thirst in the Toils.

MORAL: Promise anything; you can always repudiate.

III

THE SATYR AND THE COMMERCIAL TRAVELLER

A Satyr having met a Commercial Traveller who had lost his way in a bitter Snow Storm, took the stranger to his cave and generously gave him a warm Meal, to which he even added a large Jorum of hot Spirits-and-water. As the Traveller consumed this grateful provision in a somewhat voracious Manner, the Satyr could not restrain his native Tendency to satirize his Guest; whereupon the latter beat the Satyr most violently and turned him out of his own home into the Night to die.

MORAL: "The Guest may be witty at the expense of his Host but not the Host at the expense of his Guest," says Lady Goole in her *Etiquette Book for the Coronation Year*. She is right.

IV

THE FOX AND THE CROW

A Fox having Caught Sight of a Crow perched upon a Branch above his head with a Lump of Cheese in its Beak addressed the Carnivorous Volatile in the following Terms: "Why on Earth should you be eating Cheese? It doesn't suit you! Besides which, I can see from here it is Camembert and perfectly Crude. It might as well be Chalk." "You lie," cried the Crow excitedly, opening its Beak and letting Drop the Camembert, "it is very good Camembert. I stole it with the greatest care." "Wrong again," said the Fox as he sniffed the Article. "It is Canadian. I shall take it away to Annoy you, but I shall not Eat it."

MORAL: He who talks most talks last.

V

THE SUN, THE STORM, AND THE TRAVELLER

The Sun and the Storm having observed a Harmless Traveller footslogging it along, determined with that Detestable Malice usual among Gods, to strip him of his Coat—and they laid Bets as to which of Them would do it first. The Storm began, and naturally failed, for the Traveller only wrapped himself more closely. When the Sun took it up the Traveller was glad to find his Coat dried for nothing but, though Sweating like a Pig, would not take it off because it was such a Hell of a Bother to carry. When, however, the Weary Wayfarer perceived in the Distance up the Highway three large Gilded Balls and knew that he could get the price of several Drinks in the Neighbouring City and at the same time be lightened of his Coat, he gratefully entered the Premises of Hiram Macdonald, Licensed to Advance Money to the Unfortunate, and came out unburdened save for further Coins.

MORAL: Economic pressure will often accomplish what physical force has failed to effect.

VI

THE ANIMALS AND THEIR KING

The Animals having met in concourse to decide who should be King over them, some proposed the Lion for his Theatrical Manner and great Wig, which would impose Awe, the chief Ingredient of Sovereignty. Others preferred the Fox, whose habit of doubling, twisting, and general Sly Cunning marked him for Public Life. A large Party supported the Skunk; a still larger one the Great Three-Toed Sloth of the Andes, conceived to be free from all Tendency to Tyranny. At the end of their Debate a Jackass, prominent for the vigour of his Voice and the Representative Quality, moved a resolution that there should be no King at all, but that every Animal should do in future what he felt inclined, everywhere and at all times. This Proposition was carried by Acclamation. Whereupon the Boa-constrictor swallowed the Goat, the Hounds set upon the Fox and tore him to pieces, the Lion accounted for no less than three Antelopes before falling into a Siesta, the Cats ate the Rats and Mice, and these inoculated many with the Plague.

MORAL: Government of the people, for the people, but (above all) *by* the people.

VII

THE HUSBANDMAN AND THE VIPER

A Husbandman (Poor Devil!) having found a Viper frozen stiff in an English July, picked It up and put It in his Bosom, "For," said He, "I am credibly informed by the Gentlemen who take Large Salaries from the Royal Zoological Society, that Vipers are quite Tame and have been adopted in Pets' Corner." When the Beast thawed, It stung the Husbandman more sharply than a Thankless Child: who thereupon exclaimed: "We must reform the Civil Service in all its Branches and especially those Public Bodies which, here in Britain, escape their Responsibilities on the Pretence of Independence." Whereupon He expired in Great Agony and was buried at the Cross Roads with a Stake through his Chest.

MORAL: It is not known what happened to the Viper.

XXXIII

The Historian

WHAT is the historian?

The historian is he who tells a true story in writing.

Consider the members of that definition (which is exact and sufficient): by the consideration of each we shall be able to discover those ends which an historian should serve and the means by which he should attain them. This essential piece of thinking (essential because without record society lacks substance) we may approach before examining the motives which urge the historian to write, and only turn to these when we have assured ourselves of what his action should be.

There are in this definition four terms: first, the agent is a man; second, his act is that of telling a story, that is of recording a series of events in their consequence; third, the story he tells must be true; fourth, he tells it in writing.

I

In that he is a man it is implied that he writes for other men. Now, these others may be of his own kind, or of a different kind. He may be writing for an audience of his own experience and temper, using, to convince them of the truth, such methods as would bring conviction to himself: taking for granted that with which he is himself familiar; omitting what would be irrelevant to his own judgment. In so writing he considers only two parties to his task, himself and his matter. Or he may be writing for men so different from himself that he needs to stand outside himself, as it were, and consider his audience as a third object—himself, his narrative, and his audience being distinct in his mind.

He must, in that case, put his imagination to perpetual pains so that he shall enter into moods which are strange to him, and unceasingly consider as he writes this foreign consciousness to which he is appealing.

We find, then, at the outset, two kinds of history necessarily differing in method, though both propose to record the truth. Here, as in every other piece of analysis designed to have practical value, we must reject with contempt those sophistries of scepticism (the intellectual curse of all civilizations as they fail through age) which would pretend that no line can be drawn between the native and the alien, between the similar and the dissimilar. We must postulate common sense and agree that there is history written for our fellows, and history written for those who are not of us.

The difference between the two kinds is determined also by the nature of the story told. Thus a Catholic writing the history of the Reformation for Catholics, and writing it truly, will write it in a different fashion from the way in which he will write it for Protestants. A Protestant describing (as in that excellent book on John Knox recently appearing from the pen of Mr. Muir) a Calvinist character, to make it understood by men who have had no personal experience of Calvinism, will write differently from one who is describing the character to other Calvinists, who have passed through the same inner experiences as those which John Knox suffered or enjoyed. A Frenchman writing the history of France for his fellow countrymen, an Englishman writing the history of England for Englishmen, will be compelled to methods other than those which either would use for telling the story of his country to foreigners.

Of this duality in method we have the greatest example when a man steeped in the air of Pagan antiquity and filled with sympathy for it undertakes to present it to those minds about him, which, whether they know it or not, have been formed by a long series of Christian generations. While a converse task of perhaps greater importance to-day is imposed upon the Christian who would explain to modern minds what the full Christian culture once was: for modern minds have, in varying degrees, drifted from it.

The historian who presents his story to his own kind has clearly the simpler and by far the easier task; and it is this facility which explains the solid simplicity of all the earlier chronicles. Joinville, setting down his immortal picture of St. Louis, puts it before men who are as familiar as he himself with the arms and manners of that world. The historian writing for his own kin has only to put down in their right order those things significant to himself. In that which is the prime art of good narrative—the selection of what may be omitted—he discards without any conscious effort all that would be redundant through familiarity, and all that is of insufficient interest in his own eyes. He has but to say to himself, "What should I have wished to hear from one who had the advantage of my knowledge in this particular field?"

The great mass of good history and all bad history whatsoever is of this kind[1], written by men for an audience of their own kind. But it is the other sort, rarely indeed achieved, which does the principal work, for it is the other sort which cuts against the grain as it were, is put to a special effort, feels itself dealing with harder material, and, therefore, if successful, is productive of the more enduring result. I do not use the word "steadfast" in the sense that such work alone can survive among men, for an historical work may survive through its charm apart from its justice, and will often survive the better for repeating cherished falsehoods; but "steadfast" in the sense that a conversion, as it were of one's audience, is brought into being when one

[1] Thus nearly all our English histories are of this sort, being written by men in sympathy with the development of England since the Reformation and for an audience of their own temper. This is due to the peculiar homogeneity of modern England in fundamental religion and its social consequences. It is not so in countries where the citizens are profoundly divided on philosophy and morals.

impresses them with an unfamiliar truth. A new state of mind has been created and takes root.

There is this next consideration attaching to the fact that the historian is a man; it implies that he is writing of human things. He cannot but make men his standard. If, therefore, he pretends indifference to the sense of right and wrong which is characteristic of man, or to the sense of the comic which is characteristic of man, or to the strain between reality and the ideal which is the sense of the tragic and is also peculiar to man ("in his eyes foreknowledge of death"), or if he present a story wherein the hidden springs of action are not those which all men know to be the true springs of action determining the labours of mankind, his story is warped and bad. Thus it is that in all the great historians we discover, though more often by implication than in set phrase, the constituents of man's soul. We assist as we read them at tragedy, at comedy, at ambition, despair, and even occasional gleams of beatitude.

II

The second term of definition is the Story: that is, events in a certain consequence.

Herein we discover that essential of soundness in history, that it shall possess the mind with a reasonable process. It must establish not only the "How" but the "Why." A mere relation unconnected (however subtle and hidden the connection) by the chain of cause and effect is chaotic and inhuman, making that which in criticism we call "The Dull."

In this connection appears the truth that history is not good history unless it is readable, unless it occupies the eager and receptive soul of man as a listener. False and insufficient history may also do that. History is not sound because it is readable. But history which is not readable is not history at all.

That dense phalanx of modern academic historians whose work is as dry and dissociated, as detailed and as formless, as sawdust are, properly speaking, not historians at all; and the contempt which they too often manifest for those who possess the gifts they themselves lack is a measure of their own incapacity. It must needs be that mere detail should be accumulated without consideration of its place in the whole scale, for there must be quarrying before there is building, and there must be a carrying of bricks before there is the construction of a wall. But let not the humble multitude whose function it is to shoulder the hod set up for architects, or even for builders: they are nothing of the kind.

The story told is the more easy to tell readably when it concerns a single personality. On this account many men may attempt with some success the historical biography who have not the parts for a more general scheme. The greater the number of characters, the larger the scene; the more numerous the reactions between various motives and various material surroundings, the more difficult is the historical task. But whether that task be attempted in the limited business of biography or the large one of presenting a general pageant of affairs, two prime conditions attach to it, as they must to everything which proceeds from the creative powers of man. These two conditions are conditions of limitation: first there must be a frame, and secondly there must be that trinity which the philosopher demanded, a beginning, a middle, and an end.

History is not false but true when it is put dramatically. It is not true but false when it arrives anyhow, proceeds at random like an unconsidered run of nature, and ceases unravelled without the gathering of the threads into a conclusion. If you would set before men a just account of, say, the transformation through which our people went when they passed from the antique Paganism into the high romance of the Christian mood, you cannot but present it as a drama wherein you show an inception, an action, a conclusion arrived at. Would you describe a battle? Even though the action be inconclusive you must make its very lack of conclusion a sort of catastrophe. A river is not a river without banks, nor an object an object without contour, nor anything a thing save through form. A thing is itself because it is one; and unity—the principle of existence—will not be maintained in any story unless that story proceeds upon a plan consonant to the rational soul of man.

So let me conclude by a phrase, strange, perhaps, in modern ears. History is not history unless it be inspired with the teleological spirit, unless there be running through it an end which the whole business conspires to produce: a final cause. Let us praise, therefore, those books of history from which we rise saying to ourselves: "Now I see how that great fall came about"; or, "I am fed: for I am filled with the knowledge of how this good which I have so long admired was brought into the world, established, and completed." Even if this effect upon us is reached by a false tale, that false tale presents a quality which true tales also must have if they are to be tales at all.

But this prime character in history, that it is a story, that every effort in the writing of history must be the presentation of a dramatic action, does not mean that the action should be in that special form implied by the word "drama" used in a limited sense.

Here is a distinction subtle and difficult to follow, but unavoidably necessary to right judgment in our inquiry. To select the material in an historical presentation so that it shall lead like an acted play to a particular final scene, to omit essentials which make reality elaborate and to prefer the simplicity of a single thread to the organic complexity of life, is to fall from history into fiction. Therefore true history will never be as it were a spear thrust, but rather a piece of carving. There must be present in history the air of multitude. It must have unity: but the unity of a frieze.

The story must live, as must all stories to be stories indeed, but it must live through something manifold in the corporate actions of men rather than through that cleanly individual life which attaches to one plot and to an isolated fortune. It must live by the power of numbers, in a foison of motive and with the admission of what drama, strictly so-called, eliminates— imperfect deed, ambition half-fulfilled and half-frustrated, enigmas unsolved, contradictions unreconciled; nor, as a shallow judgment might pronounce, do such admissions destroy the strong oneness of the affair.

III

The story told must be true, and here again we will not linger upon the futility of those who are proud to publish exercises in the self-evident truth that the human mind can only perceive some infinitesimal part or fraction of reality. Here, again we use common sense, and know what we mean when we say that a relation is true or false. Let us rather admit that all men know the meaning of that word "truth" and consider what is practical to our purpose: the enemies of truth in history.

There are two such enemies, diverse in character. The one is ignorance, the other advocacy.

Ignorance is of two kinds, an ignorance of proportion and an ignorance of such facts as a sense of proportion will discover to be of primary importance.

For instance: a man who makes Drake and Hawkins the out-standing figures in the reign of Elizabeth is ignorant of right proportion. A man who sees that Cecil was the master of the time has proportion: but if he does not know that Cecil was a new man, he is ignorant of an essential fact.

All truth lies in proportion; for it is clear that complete reality cannot be known by limited beings, and that even in the most restricted field there are an infinite number (millions upon millions, and more millions of millions) of facts which the examiner of that field cannot know. Further, in what he knows selection must be made—for had you to write down the events of one waking hour in your life, with all the little that you know of cause and effect in its composition, your whole lifetime would not suffice for the task. Bad judgment—that is, a false notion—

proceeds, then, from lack of proportion. In order to make a true relation of any character or event, proportion in the factors of that event or character, the putting of the first things first and the sacrificing of the lesser to the greater, is the very maker of truth; that is, of the recognition of reality.

I see far off a tree. I say, by its shape, colour, and habit, that it is an elm. I cannot count the leaves nor distinguish them at such a distance. I come so near that I can see every leaf, yet I do not tell a greater truth nor even a fuller one by describing every leaf. It is sufficient that I repeat, "This is an elm," and proportion exists in relation to that which has been told. Again, if I am telling the true story of a crime in the discovery of which decisive events turned upon the fact that a certain tree was an elm and not an oak, then I lack proportion if I call it a "tree," at large, omitting that it was an elm. But if the events of the crime did not concern the tree at all but turned upon a particular date, then to neglect the date and to emphasize a tree in the neighbourhood for the sake of the picture only is an error in proportion: serviceable in fiction, a blemish in history. Similarly, if I am writing the military history of a battle and miss the essential manœuvres in order to give space for praising the virtue of the troops, my proportion is at fault.

Now, ignorance of proportion being the form of ignorance which most warps history, there is also that other form of ignorance that, while we recognize the first things to be first, we are not sufficiently instructed upon them. Thus I may be familiar with the truth that in the miserable decline of the English monarchy to its extinction in the seventeenth century, the chief cause was the decline of revenue due to the Crown, and the corresponding increase of income among the great landlords, who set out to kill kingship and substitute their own rule for that of the monarch. I have my proportion right. But if I have not studied what the revenue of the Crown was, nor can tell my readers why it so declined, then my approach to reality in that connection suffers from ignorance of essential fact.

If ignorance of proportion be the main form of ignorance causing false history, and ignorance of some one element, though recognized to be important, the second form, and if ignorance of either sort, or of both combined, be fatal to the historian, there is also that other worse poison, advocacy. In a society where men are trained to advocacy, and where it leads to the highest fortunes or, what is worse, to the highest repute, truth fails. It is an error that advocacy upon the one side balances advocacy on the other and that reality is found in the result of the contest. Advocacy is the negation of truth.

Now all humanity, being subject to affection, must be tempted to advocacy; and it may be justly said that every historian is in some degree affected by this vice. Yet it is true that in proportion as he escapes it is the historian worthy of his trade. Thomas Wentworth, first Lord Strafford, deserted his colleagues; having gone so far with his own class of great landlords against the power of the King of England he went no farther; he abandoned at a certain moment opposition to the Crown and engaged in that for which he knew himself to be well fitted, the active task of government. Many motives were at work upon him. The death of Buckingham (a rival and enemy) gave him his opportunity. In some degree he desired to exercise those great talents which made him chafe under the lack of opportunity. In some degree he was disgusted with the lack of sincerity and the bombastic rhetoric of such colleagues as Elliot, and reacted against them. Writing truth of that one man lies in establishing the right proportion between these diverse motives. If I fall into abusing him as a traitor, I sink to the vulgar level of Whig pamphleteering, but then if I make out all his motives good or—what is worse—pretend that their good or evil does not matter but only their efficiency for government, I am, by lack of moral proportion, falling into the opposite error; though my eulogy may not be as foolish, it is as untrue as a Whig diatribe.

Right judgment in all such matters proceeds, not from the cataloguing of the various forces at work, admitting the plus and admitting the minus, but by a combination of imagination and knowledge, getting as it were into the skin of the man so long dead, looking through his eyes and feeling his own ardours and self-reproaches, and his own self-justifications. Since you cannot judge history as God must judge it, judge it at least through the conscience which you share with all men and which is of God. But never let an historian cheat himself with the secret plea that if he by his advocacy falsifies to the left some other man will falsify to the right, and that so a balance will be struck. Let him make modification of his every phrase until the whole effect correspond to the vision of the past he has called up in his mind.

At the base of such a task there is necessary a right philosophy, and therefore is it justly said that without a true philosophy— that is, a true religion—true history cannot be written.

IV

The last member of the definition is this. The historian writes, he does not preach or sing. His function is not a function of rhetoric or poetry, it is a function of prose. But prose, perhaps the greatest of human arts, is singularly impatient of perfection. What is prose? It is the conveyance of that which is in the mind of the writer to the mind of the reader so that between the two there shall be, as much as is possible, an exact correspondence; this is what is meant by the golden definition that lucidity is the soul of prose. Herein we have one of those many cunning traps which the nature of the outer world sets for the nature of man. The inexperienced will think that to be lucid is the commonest of qualities in written expression, and that good prose or great prose is good or great through its poignancy or through the matter with which it deals, or from the violence or vividness of the picture it summons to the mind. Manifestly this is not so. Good rhetoric and good poetry are good in this fashion, but not good prose; and that prose is greatest which is most good, that is, most consonant to its end; but the end of prose is expression —nothing more. Yet how mightily difficult! See how rare are those who hardly find an obstacle to expression and in whom lucidity arises native like an inspiration!

If this be true of all prose it is true more particularly of the prose of the historian. His network of threads must never become a tangle; he cannot relieve the strain upon his pen by calling in the aid of fancy. There is ever present before him that vast inconsequence of things as they are in the real world which he must, none the less, reduce to consequence or fail in his task of telling a story. At every step will he be tempted to interpolate, to except, to weary the reader with hesitation, to attempt conviction through repetition; in no department of authorship is there so great a temptation to ease the burden by a false simplification, nor in any is there need for so multiple a grasp. It has been compared (has the writing of historical prose) to the driving of many horses in one team. It is far more involved than that! It is the driving of many horses and of some few oxen, and of here and there tigers, and of attempting to yoke with them eagles as well, so that an element of flight may be added to the strength or agility of what must tread the solid ground. With all this there is little reward for the labour done. No man perhaps has achieved fame through the telling of historical truth: no man, certainly, has achieved wealth thereby.

With that last sentence in mind, let me conclude with a brief consideration of what I said at my outset I would postpone: the matter of motive.

Why, then, do men write history? If it is as advocates, they are, as historians, worthless. If it is to excite strong feeling through their craft as does the poet or the rhetorician, they are the less historians. If it is to show their skill in the solution of problems, they are beneath the level of their calling and resemble men who, having the duty of defending their honour by the sword, think rather of how they shall be praised for their fencing.

The true spring of action for the historian is this: that there lies in man a certain God-given necessity for communicating to his fellow-men that reality of which he has become possessed. Just as God (if the word may still be used) has put it into the hearts, especially of young men, to desire fame, in order that the work of the world may be done, and has spurred on with other necessities lovers, martyrs, and sailors to new worlds, so in this poor but noble sobriety of history you have an inspiring force. It is the inspiration not of fame nor of this human ideal or that vision of the divine. It is only the inspiration of the thing discovered, urging its human instrument to give it outward expression and to establish it in the general mind.

Nor let it be forgotten that there is mixed up with this strong and permanent motive a motive of civic virtue. For history is to society what memory is to a man, and only by true record do nations know themselves.

XXXIV

Sussex the Resistant

THE County of Sussex has this peculiarity among all the counties of England: that it is more resistant than any. The test is applied to it because it is the nearest to London of the maritime counties on the Channel. Under modern circumstances it has been under more danger of swamping than any other of the old native and traditional districts, and yet it has resisted.

It has always had this quality. It was a separate kingdom much later than any other county; indeed, it was in this unique: remaining a district ruled by one man until far into the Dark Ages, and that was a system originating at least with the Romans, and perhaps earlier. To this day it is co-terminous with its Bishopric, and one may talk a little fantastically but without too much exaggeration of "the Kingdom of Sussex."

This quality of resistance it preserved for two thousand years. The Reformation affected it late, save in the seaport towns, which were everywhere the first open to new influences. Within the county the older mediæval traditions of life lingered far on, even up to 1745. It similarly preserved beyond any other districts, save those of the remote west and north, its original habits in agriculture, in building, and in forestry. Though it was on the high road from the Channel to the Capital, though it had been traversed by armies perpetually throughout the Middle Ages, though it was in the sixteenth, seventeenth, and eighteenth centuries a centre of iron foundry, it preserved its individual character in an astonishing degree.

When we ask what was the cause of this isolation, I think we shall find the answer in two material causes, and one moral cause—which last we cannot analyse. The material causes are the clay of the Weald, coupled with the fact that the clay rises high and is singularly unfruitful. The moral cause would seem to lie in something of the local character which opposes an obstinate front to change. The grassland of the chalk Downs, the very fertile sea-plain, the equally fertile belt of loam to the north of the Downs, were each productive of human wealth in sheep and wheat and pasturage, and all that men need. Therefore, Sussex had a local prosperity of its own; yet was it cut off from the rest of England by the great expanse of marsh round about Rye to the east, and the corresponding marshy inlets of the sea from Chichester harbour to Portsmouth on the west. During the Dark Ages the county was further cut off by the breakdown of the bridges, over its small but muddy and difficult rivers; notably by the breakdown of the Roman bridge across the Arun at Alfoldean.

Sussex was the last county to become Christian and civilized. Sussex was kept as a sort of "native state" under the first Roman administration. Sussex was very slow to accept the changes of the Reformation, and Sussex has been equally stubborn and tenacious in its resistance to every other change, even those of our own time. I have read with amusement of a local meeting, held, I think, at Petworth, in the midst of the nineteenth century and protesting against the driving of a railway from London to Portsmouth, at a time when the rest of the country was already a network of railways. We have always been thus; and the proof of that character lies in the scores of the unchanged Sussex villages with their unaltered churches, in the hundreds of Sussex steadings of their own kind, so that any Sussex man seeing them in a picture, though he might not know the place itself, at once recognizes his home.

The division of Sussex into West and East is not modern. West Sussex has a unity of its own, geographical and historical, and although this division was only confirmed in administration (if I remember right) by the County Council Act of a generation ago, it has been potentially present ever since this highly distinct division of England came into existence.

The county is very long and narrow; it is much narrower in social reality than it seems upon the map. For if you will mark the density of population, you will perceive under modern conditions the big towns making a string along the sea coast, the lesser market-towns of the interior, and then north of these (north, that is, of Horsham to Petworth and such) a belt of sparsely inhabited territory, which is the high clay Weald dividing Sussex from Surrey. Crawley is an exception, because Crawley was something of an "annexation" from Surrey during the Middle Ages. The natural boundary of Sussex runs south of Crawley along the forest ridge; but the lords of the southern castles were wealthier than those of the Surrey castles, and extended their hunting rights by dominance in one or two places beyond the ridge, of which the Crawley district is one. Sussex therefore, especially in the state wherein it stood for century after century before the modern development of communications, was a very long thin belt. Any man could cross it on foot in a day. A man could not even ride along it in one day, and he could hardly walk it in four.

Now, it is the nature of long thin districts to split into two halves, and if they lie from east to west to split into an Eastern and a Western; because, in the administration of such, your radius of action produces at once two poles, one for the thither half and one for the hither. An order sent out from Chichester, or, better, from Arundel, by a man on horseback, would be received within the same day throughout the whole of West Sussex. An order sent out from Hastings, or, better, from Hurstmonceaux, would be received in the same day throughout East Sussex.

There was never a formal distinction until quite recent times, but it is significant that Chichester was the Bishop's town, Lewes the centre of the civil administration.

But the distinction between West and East Sussex goes much deeper than the mechanical effect of the county's outline. There is a real difference in landscape, and therefore in value.

An old and valued neighbour of mine, himself a squire of West Sussex (now dead) whose conservatism was of that intense and fiery sort which is by far the best, said to me once in my early manhood: "Have you ever been to a place called East Sussex?" I said I had; that I used to go and visit near Roberts-bridge in my childhood, and that afterwards I had gone to see Coventry Patmore, the poet, in Hastings, sent there by my mother when I was a lad.

To this the old squire made answer: "It is a most extraordinary place! I went there once on a driving tour with my wife. . . . It is really a most astounding place!"

Now, I know that this anecdote (which is rigidly true) may be regarded as a piece of affectation by people who think in larger units; for, after all, the old gentleman was talking of a place only one long day's ride away; but his feeling was per-fectly genuine and exactly corresponded to reality.

If I were asked what were the most distinctive tests between the east and the west of Sussex, I should say, the shape of the inland hills. The chalk downs, indeed, run on from the west into the east, and do not fall into the sea until they are well past the Ouse and even the Cuckmere, at Beachy Head; but when you get north of these you see the difference at once. The lines of West Sussex are long lines like those of waves following on a wind. The lines of East Sussex are sharp, pyramidal, isolated, pointed: Heathfield, Mayfield, and the rest. The landscape cor-respondingly differs. The men of West Sussex will tell you, when they choose to be articulate (and they can be articulate when they choose), that their landscape is the most subtle in the world; but the landscape of East Sussex is quite clearly apparent and needs no mental digging to understand it. I should say, for my part, that the vision of South England most enduring and most reposeful, and perhaps the most fruitful in any man's mind, is that over the valley of the lower Arun, seen from the height of the road between Storrington and Amberley, looking west-ward. It has been a little interfered with by modern council cottages, but Sussex is doing to those cottages what it has done to everything so far—it is taming them; and for the rest, you have an expanse of hill pasture and water and wood wherein there lives a certain spirit, which I will not attempt to describe, but which *IS*. Now, if you will look over a belt of East Sussex, as, for instance, from Crowborough Top, or from Brightling, it is another matter. Anybody could understand it. I do not say that in its dispraise, but at any rate is is true: anybody could understand it. It is striking. West Sussex is not striking. It is revealing. Put me by Byworth looking southward towards Gumber Corner and Duncton Hill, and you are giving me an ante-chamber to Paradise. I do not find such things east of Wolstonbury. I have permanently inhabiting my mind that view on which I so often dwelt in my boyhood, from the pines of Crowborough Top (which was then deserted and almost unknown) towards Firle. But it is not the same thing as the view from Byworth. If I may say so without affectation, it has no irony. But in my own part of the county there is irony, which is that of some spirit, saying: "All this is yours for ever, but you will not possess it long."

I think it may be made a test of the fortunes of England whether Sussex will continue to resist, or no. The Norman and the Angevin armies, the storm of the sixteenth century, the Civil Wars, passed over it and left it the same. The railways bred on it those huge suburbs of London: which are the sea-coast towns, notably Brighton. But within my own memory Sussex was Sussex within three miles of Brighton: and I have watched the rabbits playing at evening within a hundred yards of the Brighton road.

Steam did not kill Sussex; nor did the bicycle—of which so many evil things were prophesied. Will petrol kill it?

I don't know. I hope not . . . but I don't know.

XXXV

The Barbarians

IT is a pity that true history is not taught in schools. If it were, people would understand much better the history of what is passing in their own time. For instance, the dangers which are now threatening European civilization are of the same sort *in part* with those which threatened and at last undermined the old pagan civilization of Rome.

That civilization was not destroyed by invaders, it was never defeated in any decisive battle. What happened to it was that it was undermined from within, and it was undermined from within by very much the same forces which are destroying the supports of our own traditional culture. Those forces are the forces of contrast between well-being and indigence, coupled with the contrast between freedom and servitude and enforced by the contrast between human and inhuman relations. When a large number of men are compelled to labour by a small number of men, when their labour is passed under inhuman conditions and the sense of servitude inseparable from the *enforcement* of labour in any form, they end by driving the masses subject to such disabilities to rise against their wrongs. But in doing this, the rebels may well act blindly, for the very conditions of their subjection forbid them the culture that would enable them to act wisely. They are impelled not only by the desire for freedom but by the hatred of those who exploit them and who enjoy a freedom of security and substance denied to themselves. They are filled also with a general hatred; a love of destruction for its own sake.

The pagan empire, from which we are all descended, was accumulating these same evils in its old age. The social form was different, but the spiritual reactions were much the same. The number of free men grew less, the number of men in slavery grew greater; even the free, all save the most privileged, grew more and more embarrassed. The organized armed force upon which everything depended was more and more recruited from men not possessed of the full Roman civilization, but either born outside the boundaries of the Empire or settled within them and yet not fully digested into the general culture. Soldiers of such a kind tended to take things more and more into their own hands and be officered by people like themselves. The men who watched the general breakdown of society in the West saw what was passing before them as a social revolution—and they were right.

We to-day in what used to be Christendom are slipping down the same slope. Our leaders grow more indifferent to culture, the organized masses grow less susceptible to the leadership of men trained in a high tradition, the area of freedom grows rapidly less, the great mass of men suffer an increasingly servile condition. The relation between the mass of men and their labour is inhuman and the relation between the mass of men and their economic masters has also lost its old human savour. Men will accept subjection when it is connected with loyalty and humour and the air of domesticity; they will not accept it when it is mechanical and therefore hopeless.

But though the parallel between our present entry into general revolution is singularly like the entry of our fathers into the Dark Ages, there is one most disturbing difference between the two tragic epochs, making our peril far more tragic than theirs.

This difference does not come from the triumphs of what is called "Science" in the art of destroying mankind, nor does it lie in the use of this or that instrument of war. It was possible to exterminate one's fellow beings by the myriad and to un-people the whole of a vast country when men had nothing more than bows and arrows and sharp blades to do it with. Mesopotamia was thus destroyed.

No, the difference between our father's entry into their Dark Ages and our own is this: there inhabited an increasing number of men during the fourth and fifth centuries a certain spirit or philosophy which was capable of saving all that could be saved of the old culture. There was a new religion abroad—well-organized, universal, and definite. By this instrument our civilization was saved half-way down the slope. It did not recover the fullness of its ancient glory, but it survived and rose again after a long ordeal of nearly five hundred years. The eleventh century was a daybreak, and the twelfth was a morning, and the thirteenth was a glorious day.

We have with us now no such saving influence. There is, indeed, a sort of new miasmic philosophy drifting about, but it is morally of the basest and intellectually contemptible, not even capable of definition. It will not be able to insure its own survival as a mood, let alone the survival of our inheritance. You may see its fruits in the works of modern men: their building, their daubs, their obscenity of prose, their deafness to harmony and rhythm, and their blindness to beauty. We of to-day have no chance of survival, save by reaction, by the restoration of ancestral things. But among these we must include a passion for social justice and an establishment of human relations between man and man. Otherwise we shall not only perish but perish in hypocrisy, and therefore in despair.

XXXVI

The Test is Poland

THE phrase which stands as the title of this leading article is one that I have used myself over my own signature more than once. It is the most obvious and important of all political truths connected with the present struggle. It is also the one most difficult for the public in this country to appreciate. If the Allies succeed in restoring a free and strong Poland with full access to the sea through ports attached to the Polish state, they have won the war. If, through misunderstanding the problem, they accept a peace of any kind, no matter how complete in appearance, which still leaves the fate of Poland undecided, the Allies have quite certainly lost the war.

A free and sufficiently independent Polish state is the condition of civilized Western influence in Central Europe. It is the necessary counterbalance to the Prussian spirit, which will endure east of the Elbe even if it be exorcised from the rest of the Germans. The first partition of Poland was the beginning of all our troubles. It put barbarism back into Christendom; it admitted, for the first time in our history, without shame and without reason, the brutal denial of international law and of a Christian nation's right to live. The two villains of the piece were exactly what they are to-day: the Russian Government and the upstart and impossible power of Prussia. The Imperial House at Vienna was over-persuaded by its advisers, and allowed itself to become a reluctant and minor partner in the crime. There was some good in this evil, for it introduced into the control of Poland a civilized note, and permitted some survival of a maimed Polish liberty upon the extreme upper basin of the Vistula, where Cracow remained the symbol of Polish political life.

Whether the great Christian Empress could have enforced her desire to refuse participation in the evil act it is difficult to say; at any rate, she did not refuse. She contented herself with saying that posterity would pay dearly for that defiance of all European and Christian tradition. She was right. Posterity *has* paid dearly; for on the ruins of Poland the last stage of Prussian power arose, and it was the first attack on Poland more than anything else, which confirmed Berlin in its belief that no divine vengeance awaits iniquity.

If history were taught among us; if our governing class were given in youth some general idea of what Europe is, of how Europe arose and how Europe may die—or were even made to understand that England is a province of Christendom and of Europe and that, with the failure of the West, England quite certainly goes under—the essential importance of Poland at this moment would be grasped by those who conduct our destinies. As it is, very few know so much as the meaning of Poland, its religion, and its resistance. They know all about the defects and the weakness, they know nothing about the heroism and the tenacity. In so far as they have vaguely heard the name "Poland," it suggests to them something like the name "Ireland." To say that is enough.

It may be too late to awake opinion at all to the key position of Poland in the present mortal struggle. It may be that, through the impossibility of teaching men who have no grounding in the past, the fatal compromise will be carried out which will mean that the West is defeated.

There is, I repeat (and I care not how often it has to be repeated since repetition is the only form of argument modern men in our urban decay can understand)—there is one central criterion of value and success: the resurrection of Poland.

When we wrote here in the critical days of last summer that the failure to control Danzig would ultimately mean the failure to control British predominance in Asia, we wrote something which was one aspect of the central truth on Poland. But in whatever aspect or form this truth is emphasized, it *must* be acted upon, unless we prefer to accept rapid and final decline. Poland is the test.

The determination to save Poland, which is a determination not only to defeat Prussia but to oust the vile and murderous Communism of Moscow, is the moral condition of victory.

If we waver we are lost.

[From *The Weekly Review*, January 4th, 1940. The paper is now defunct.]

XXXVII

Tender Farewell to the World

MUST I then leave you, deep woods that overhang slow rivers and pastures in between? I know a place in Normandy (or knew it once upon a time) where food was served to the wanderer-by upon the terrace of an old stone house which overlooked the broad and peaceful flood from beneath such trees; there could he sit and hold communion with the pleasant things of this world and with the promise of much more. For the forest made a screen for him miles deep covering the hills. The river was his moat. Along the ancient highway by the farther shore slow carts would move drawn by contented, powerful horses with their contented master walking at their side.

There was another place also, near a northern English shore, where wolds almost innocent of man stood up against the sky, and in between ran a torrent brown after rain, breaking over granite, smooth granite. There, save for the noise of the waters, nothing was heard. Up that glen also ran a road; but none came along it hour after hour. A powerful solitude, alive with the puissance of the hills, controlled the majestic simplicity all around. There also, from the morning to the evening of the summer's day, alone, a man could become part of that magnitude by which we were made and in which reposed the awful borderland.

And must I leave you, hills and rivers, must I leave you, that brown water of the Northumbrian dale and that calm Norman land?

Must I leave you also, small ancient cities of delight, multiple, filled with a traditional glory, exhibiting in a hundred corners of carved stone the delight my fellows before me had in the business of this world and in the spirit of their province and in the humour of coming and of going, of leaving and of arriving, of the market? Your walls remained. Sometimes they were all about you like a girdle, at others they were loosened by ruins. Their bastions recalled, this one the first artillery, that the violent colour of the old horseback wars, another the strength of the dark ages in which stone was like the rock whence it was hewn, and the battlements were like cliffs raised in the days when men knew not or disdained ornament; in another gateway an arch proclaimed the decay of the Empire; in another survived some small and venerable fragment of the Roman time.

You little cities all up and down the world, habitations of Christian men, with your small palaces that had seen a thousand uses and were here museums, there town halls, and in more than one still gave a roof to the descendants of your original lords; must I leave you?

Must I leave you, my innumerable little towns, my endless rosary of little towns; my towns of Italy and of the Germanies and of Poland and of France and Spain? Must I leave you for good and all?

Must I leave you, too, strong debates of mind with mind and bolting out of truth; conversations of men?

Carousals nourished with all the liquors of man's invention, from the Grampians to the sands south of Atlas, intensified by quarrel, blown through with laughter, lifted by sudden perceptions; discussions, symposia, seed-plots of discovery and nurseries of inspiration, commerce of souls; must I leave you also, or at least leave you in the only setting I have ever known? Must I leave the doubtful, the unconcluded, the creative question and answer, proper to mortal men in this portentous little life they have to live, their wayfaring almost infinite in its horizon, their pilgrimage too, unsatisfied? Must I leave you, arguments?

Must I leave you also, conflicts, enmities, challenges? Am I no more to feel the stubborn resistance of the animal's will nor my own strict pleasure in its containment, the guiding of the rein, the pressure of the knee? And must I leave you also, most noble of certamina, the encounter with the sea?

Must I never more communicate through the tiller with the life of the hull and with the God that is in the wind upon the sail, nor hold her plunging any more into the exultant water, nor any more make with a fixed gaze for the mark far away upon the headland over the edge of the world: the headland that might be a low cloud save that it does not move: the headland behind which are the stone piers and the sheltered water and the roofs of home?

Must I leave you, innumerable records of men, and my own poor delight—but delight—in addition thereto; the written word and the silent sound of it in the mind, the rhythm of English and the idea taking on form and being?

It is said that all companionships are grievous to lose, and that while all good things must end, of all good things the hardest to abandon are the intimate companionships of solitude, the companionships of the soul, books made or making.

When I have read the writings of some man long dead, a great poet or a master satirist proclaiming the glory of God, my mind has taken on an amplitude to which it seems hardly native; I grew beyond my boundaries, I became by communion a part of that which I received, and thenceforward I moved, not a companion of, nor even an heir to, but a very participant in, the epics and the feasts, the discoveries, the altitudes, the revelations of so great a company. One might marvel how man ever achieved so much by letters and could so multiply and extend himself and spread outwards into perpetual new fields of achievement. If we have been of the poets and of the prophets in this fashion, can we bear to be rid of that magnitude—must we say, even to that, good-bye—and for ever?

And our own verses, our own delight in expression concluded and in the accomplished magic, must that also be left aside, put away, abandoned?

Halls of old time, colonnades, and domes of the rebirth of

Europe, temples of the antique gods and visions rising above these, tiers of resplendent marble, great flights of steps cascading and broadening down as they descend from hillsides to the lakes of Lombardy, or cypress walks of the Imperial villas, or feasting rooms of the great kings; and all the pictured things and all the sculptured things; the heavenly head just barely tinted, almost translucent, bending downward in alabaster, saved miraculously from the buried city in the Albanian hills; the Etruscan tombs and the majesty of the dead reclining upon their couches of stone with faces still full of command and proclaiming perpetually the business of life and of death—those Etruscan tombs under the volcanoes which had nourished so great a people, and from whose dust still springs the grape which perpetuates their genius, Corneto, city of graves and immortality, must these also be left behind?

The greater mountains, wherein sublimity so much excels our daily things, that in their presence experience dissolves, and we seem to enter upon a kind of eternity—must so much majesty be relinquished, and must we turn back from it and go away ungratefully as from lords to whom we have grown disloyal? Must we have done for ever with those immeasurable deeps into whose vastness we were by our littleness absorbed? Must I no more catch my breath at seeing, revealed beyond the clouds above me, a living spear of light which was the suddenly apparent ice of the summit? Are the mountain paths never again to be known by me and that approximation to the heavens?

But must I leave you also, best things of all, which are the clothing and extension of the soul itself, the things of home; the walls and the roof and the furniture of man's life? You, my habitations . . . must I leave you, fields all about, and most familiar slopes low and far against the southern sky? Must I leave you, mundane fulfilment? Yes, I must leave you all.

* * *

Well, you will be sorry to hear it, my hearties, but I leave you with no regret.

Time was, when the parting from such companions and in such numbers would have been something of a wrench; but not to-day, cullies! Not to-day! To-day I can leave you sincerely and with an open face. As times now are we can say, "Well, good-bye! So long!" and almost forget whether we have shaken hands or no. For you hills, you rivers, you horses, you boats, you woodland paths and mountain paths and paths of every other kind; you lakes, you pastures, you God-knows-what, you are all spoilt beyond redemption, and no wise man can find any use for you any more.

You have lost your dignity and your quiet, you have lost your men, not all as yet quite dead, but shattered; you are become rubbish; you are a scrap-heap; you are an offence.

Were it not in the nature of things that I must leave you I would even be at the pains of buying an enormous broom and sweeping you all aside.

And that, I beg you note, oh mountains, applies also to you, no matter how high you be or what airs you put on, or what clothing you affect of mist and precipice—and I know not what and all. It applies also to you, once dear and still familiar things, it applies to the wrestling of mind with mind—conversation is ruined like the rest, and of debate there is none left.

It is one thing to leave a feast at its height, to be compelled to break away from friends in the midst of their happiness and of our own; it is another to get off with relief from an empty hall where the lights are extinguished save for one poor ugly, naked bulb, hanging by a fly-blown wire near the office door, while a lousy serf, eager to be off to his gutter-joys, bawls, "Time, gentlemen, time," through the deserted hotch-potch of dirty table-cloth, broken glass, and stale tobacco.

Oh yes, good-bye—world—good-bye; and a good riddance of you. As for that house of stone under the Norman forest beside the meadow overlooking the river, it is now built in jazz, all zig-zags, and the food they give you is chemical, out of a tin; and they give it to you with insults, and the wine is vinegar—synthetic at that. And the road on the farther bank is a highway of hell, straight as doom, black in colour and screaming with machines, which tear past filled with Rastaqueres and their whores (by your leave—not by theirs), shooting from their clots in the vile cities to their still viler clots in the casinos which defile the oily sea. I say oily—yes, oily—the shores of the sea have become great patches of oil, sheeny with changing colours like a dying snake, and grit floats on them.

As for you, boat, you too are now peevish for a machine, you want to have a mechanism inside you instead of a soul; there is no god in your sail, for it is not a sail any longer, but a beastly triangle called a Bermuda. Time was we did put up a triangular sail when it blew so abominably that a human mainsail could not stand. But we were honest about it, we did it for an exception and out of necessity—but to sail all your life with a thing like that, and one that does not reef but rolls up on a spring, I thank you for nothing! Nay, there is something worse, it has no rings up the mast, it runs up a sort of groove like the things with which they fasten the vanity-bags of the ladies— God bless them, or curse them, I cannot decide and care not which.

You also, carousals, I will deal faithfully with you. There is none left who can sustain an argument, thinking is out of fashion, and expression died this ten years since and will not be disturbed in its grave. For accompaniment, when men would drink together, there is tinned music, grating with a damnable sound and turning upon nigger rhythms—written not even by niggers, but by Bessarabian Jews. And for converse and commerce of the mind, there are short ejaculations, principally "What?" These at the hundredth grow intolerable.

And you, my little cities, you are in my mind all right, but nowhere else. You have gone to Paradise, I suppose, whither I hope soon to follow you; certainly you are not to be found on this earth any more. Some of you are in ruins through war and no man regrets you, others they are pulling down as fast as they can; others have grown a leprous growth or fungoid excrescence of houses everywhere beyond their limits, spawning and weltering so that they have no longer boundary or unity of personality or name. Others, and of these the tragedy is deepest, are preserved in death, and their rigid charms are shouted and bawled from hoardings, and cartloads of devils come to them in rattling, hammering machines of the pit, visiting them hour after hour, day after day, with no purpose and no meaning. Better disappearance than such torture places as these.

Those ancient palaces, those antique carvings, those inhabited stones of recollection, innumerable generations of men; those memorials of my fathers that were also my fellows, things that enlarged me and were also my possession—you are a myriad banal postcards now; and those of you that will not serve that purpose are chipped away to make room for more horrors. But in some of you, under the light of glass so coloured that it is murder, processions of damned souls pass through day after day, listening to the droning of a guide who tells them lies, and unimportant lies, which they swallow with fish-mouths—half open; and with fish-eyes—half dead. Go your way—go your way—go your way.

But you books, you pens, you paper, you all the apparatus of the Muses, you baggage of Apollo (and by the way—are the Muses baggages of Apollo? But I will not digress), you do I leave with a more hearty contempt than all the rest. Home has been turned into a factory; the cars go rattling, dashing, banging, buzzing, and hurtling past; the candles are put out, and blinding, mechanical light has taken their place; there is no oil in the lamp any more, nor any lamp for that matter; there are no hangings about our beds, no worked stuff upon our walls. Home being home, to leave even the dead skeleton of home is grievous, but not to leave you—oh books, oh paper, oh ink, oh pen, oh apparatus of the Muses! Contrariwise, I say farewell to you with a more complete relief than to any other of the broken things.

The glories of the past are destroyed, they are no longer understood, and language is forgotten. Letters, you have gone down in a cataract from depth of folly to further depth, from obscenity to obscenity, until you have reached the inane. For whom should any man now write? What ears remain to hear?

Immortality

PEOPLE to-day are perpetually rediscovering very old things. That is natural, I suppose, to an epoch of discovery, though I confess I should be better contented if they would only be humble enough to surmise at least that certain ideas were very old and not suddenly sprung from their own creative brains. Thus the discussion on evolution which is as old as the human race, or at any rate as old as all recorded history of human reasoning, is beginning at last to be treated as something worth handling, and not merely a thing to be making violent affirmations about. Again the infinitely old discussion upon the modes of human government is becoming popular. People no longer simply take it for granted throughout Europe that democracy must be the best; and even those who do think it the best are beginning, at long last, to ask what democracy is.

Now, among the old things thus recently discovered, and therefore seemingly novel—novel at least to the more backward brains of Europe—is the discussion upon human immortality. It is fair to smile at those who, coming abruptly upon such hoary debates, believe themselves to be pioneers. It is fair enough to laugh at such a mixture of vanity and ignorance. But the laughter leads nowhere. It is our business rather to convince error than to scorn it.

I should think it probable that this discussion on human immortality was the very oldest present among men, from the day men, through whatever accident, either lost full knowledge or began to discuss what they did not fully know. For though we have plenty of evidence which makes it look as though man had always envisaged a life of some kind after death (evidence drawn from prehistoric remains and the more doubtful analogies of primitive people), yet in the nature of things there can be no prehistoric evidence upon the *denial* of survival. You can dig up ornaments buried with the dead; you cannot dig up the sneers of those who said that such rites were futile. And as for evidence drawn from primitive races, it is not wholly satisfactory for two reasons: first, that among not a few there is little, and among some, apparently, no idea of survival; secondly, that, after all, they have been as long on the earth as we have, and have had plenty of time to develop illusions.

But we have very old records of the debate in the shape of words written down, long after the inception of such ideas, but clearly stretching back to the beginning of inquiry; and the moment we can fully observe men going thoroughly into the affair, we find the two schools—those who accept and those who deny survival—whether among the Asiatic philosophers or the Western. On the one side: "We do not die but are changed." On the other: "It shall be with us as though we were not."

Well, then, there is nothing new about the arguments pro and con; but that does not detract from their importance, and I propose here to set out as briefly as I can what those arguments seem to me to be.

In the first place I am bound, writing as a Catholic, to define the Catholic position, but of course with this proviso, that I do not expect that position to have influence upon those who are not of my communion. The Catholic believes in the immortality of the human soul (and, for that matter, in the very existence of the human soul) on Authority. He may, indeed, discover the truth of Immortality by the use of his unaided reason, but in the main he believes it because he is told it is true by the voice of the Church; which, when it defines any one of the comparatively few but tremendous things which it has defined, is for him the voice of God. He is more certain of this than of anything except his own existence. He relies upon that Authority as the saintly old Bible Christian nurse who brought me up relied upon the literal Authority of James I's English Bible.

Having concluded by the use of observation and reason that the Church has this supreme power and right to teach, I accept what she teaches and trust her more than I do the evidence of my senses. Whether I can *imagine* the thing believed or not is to me of no intellectual consequence at all.

But, I repeat, no one who is not a Catholic can be expected even to consider that position. If I am arguing whether an out-line seen from far off at sea is a cloud or an island, I must not argue from the map if the man with whom I am arguing begins by telling me that he thinks the map has been made up out of somebody's head and that, therefore, he will not accept its evidence. I might add, before leaving this point, that we Catholics believe our authority to be Divine from observation and reason, because it fits in with every other thing that we know; while others reject what does not fit in with some preconceived theory on cause and effect.

It is the old opposition between the Catholic attitude of Faith based upon Reason and the anti-Catholic attitude of Reason based upon Faith. For our opponents—especially the scientific sceptics—must admit (if they closely analyse their own position) that their supposed certitudes are arrived at by the use of Reason based upon Faith: a blind faith in their particular philosophy of cause and effect.

But to press this most interesting point would be to enter into the whole dialogue between the Catholic and non-Catholic position, and I am here dealing with a much more particular matter.

What are the general arguments for and against the survival of bodily death by human personality?

We must begin by observing that the arguments against such survival are very strong.

I say nothing about the supposed argument from our new knowledge of the human frame. Any clear thinker can see that no amount of further accumulated detail in physical observation can add to the overwhelming physical fact apparent to all, ignorant or learned, that when the body is dead it is dead. No new specialized knowledge on the brain, for instance, can tell us more than men have always known: to wit, that "if the brains are out, the man is dead." Let us discard such irrelevant stuff and turn to the real arguments.

St. Thomas Aquinas, as was his wont in dealing with these awful matters, has summed up in the tersest and most pregnant form the three main groups of arguments which all men naturally entertain, and upon which the deniers of immortality continually rely (you will find them in the Sixth Article of the Seventy-fifth Question of the *Summa*). I will give them here, not in his order, but in the order in which they appeal most to my contemporaries.

First, there is the undoubted truth that the soul exists in thinking. Now we think wholly under physical conditions. We cannot think without physical images in our minds; we receive all the food for thought through our senses. When, therefore, we are no longer in a position to do this, when physical conditions have ceased, thinking ceases; and, supposing a permanent cessation, the soul is not.

Next, whatever came out of nothingness may return to nothingness. Modern men do not put it that way, but they continually use the argument in another form. Our consciousness came out of unconsciousness. It "developed" (as we say in modern language) out of an unconscious condition. Therefore it should reasonably return to that condition, or at least there would seem to be no reason why it should not.

But the third argument (which is the first in St. Thomas's order) is that which appeals most strongly to my contemporaries, I think, and this is, that things of a like origin and a like mode of action have presumably a like end. Our generation, our maintenance of life, are on the same model as those of the vegetable or the beast, or any other living thing. They grow old and decay, and so do we. They disintegrate to exist no longer; so shall we. And he quotes those powerful Scriptural words:

"Man has nothing more than the beast . . . the death of man and beast is one, and the condition of both is equal."

To these arguments the great philosopher adds elsewhere another which I for myself find to be of most powerful effect, though it is not in tune with the language of to-day. He points out that a thing is what it is on account of a union between matter and form. Thus a vase is what it is, not because of its material, clay, but because of its material having had added to it a certain character of shape, content, etc.; its *form* makes it a vase. Destroy the union of matter and form and the vase disappears. Crush it to powder and it is a vase no more. But the soul is the form of the body. A man is what he is by his character: his thoughts, his inward disposition, and all that makes a self out of his mere flesh. Become a corpse, the form has disappeared; of that material, flesh, the essential to making of it a man exists no more.

This is the argument on which Mr. Shaw relied in his example of the Brick in a recent letter.

Now what are the counter arguments?

In the first place, emphasize this—that without faith not one of them is conclusive in all men's eyes. They are converging. They create an increasing probability. They do not establish certainty for all men.

Before dealing with them, it is well to brush aside the commoner kinds of support. Thus the idea that a belief in immortality is a consolation, though perhaps an indication of truth, is worthless for intellectual conviction. To trust in "consolations" alone is as base intellectually as taking drugs and as worthless. It would be a consolation to an embarrassed man to foster the illusion that he was about to inherit a fortune, but he does well to avoid such self-deception. Moreover, the popular conception that survival necessarily involves happiness is intellectually negligible. Regarded in itself, apart from other considerations, it may be happy, unhappy, or neither.

No, the strong arguments are of another kind, and for my

part, though I will hardly affirm it (for no one can judge himself apart from his own experience), I should imagine that they would suffice to establish my judgment, even without that altogether stronger foundation, accepted doctrine.

The first is the nature of man, which we all feel ourselves, which we all observe in others, and from which we cannot get away. He is not on the scale of this earth. He is paradoxically at once lower and higher than what is around him. He is also, or can be also, worse and better, and that in a different mode from what is around him.

All philosophies (it is the universal burden of Pascal, among a host of profound thinkers) are founded upon either the misery of man or his greatness—or, indeed, in the case of one philosophy (but only of one, the Christian), upon the reconciliation of that greatness and that misery. Start out with a conviction of man's greatness, not necessarily subject to misery on this earth, and sooner or later you will find that you are deceiving yourself. Facts are against you. Start out with his miserable subjection, denying his super-mundane greatness, and you will find the same. He is not a beast, yet he suffers here not only more but more radically than the beasts. He is not here beatified, yet he feels capable of complete felicity. On that I think we are all agreed.

Now, if this nature of man, with the moral sense for its most active expression, is of such a sort, how can you fit it in with man as nothing but an animal on this earth?

By whichever facet you look at it, either by the commonest facet of remedy for injustice, or by that which used to be a common aspect a generation ago, of reward and punishment for good and evil deeds, or by considering the magnitude of your subject—and there are hundreds of other angles—you come back to the truth that man is not here in his element.

The second strong argument, which converges upon this first, is the argument from personality; conscious intelligent personality. That quality in man by which he is not only conscious but can stand outside his own consciousness, compare ideas, and deal with conceptions not subject to space and time.

Now we know that personality is more than non-personality. The greater does not come out of the lesser save by addition. You cannot get a quart out of a pint bottle. Only Personality will produce personality, something more personal, perhaps, but not less. Admitting personality in man, personality is behind the universe. The process of the universe has a meaning, the end of man becomes rational. But if his end is upon this earth, that end is not rational in the ultimate sense of the word "rational." It does not complete his being. It leaves not only loose ends, but loose ends of infinitely greater import than the woven strands which build up his earthly life.

That is how I see the affair. I admit I am handicapped in putting it abstractedly, because I accept it, not as an abstraction but as part of a Divine philosophy wherein all is at accord. I feel, under the effect of the Faith, not only with emotion, but by the process of all my being and especially with the lucid cogitative part of myself, two great quotations, centuries old, often recited triumphantly in song; with these I will end.

The first runs:

> *Coheredes et sodales . . .*
> *In terra viventium.*

The second:

> *Qui vitam sine termino*
> *Nobis donet in patria.*

So they stand in what was once the universal language of our civilization. In our modern local language they mean:

The first: "Co-heirs and barrack-room companions in the land of living men."

The second: "Who shall give us life without end in Our Own Country."